Acclaim for **Blanche McCrary Boyd's**

The Redneck
Way of Knowledge

"A potent presence. . . . Boyd's writing declares a voice and a sensibility, a way of seeing and thinking that is fresh and that engages us. With a rare blend of humor, affection and startling honesty, she confronts the full range of what's going on around her." —*San Francisco Chronicle*

"Boyd is a fine writer of striking, ironic wit, and she possesses a shrewd talent for sniffing out character and regional nuance. Her quest to rediscover the South comes alive." —*Philadelphia Inquirer*

"Wonderful. . . . The strength of these powerful essays is Boyd's ability to perform open-head surgery, to show us that self with high good humor and consistent candor." —*Los Angeles Times*

"Blanche Boyd is one of the intellectual roughs, with no deceptive surface, no voice but her own. The lessons she teaches us are honest, the prose in which she embeds them is funky, spare, bare-faced plain talk. She is patriotically Southern, deeply faithful to her sprawling family, instinctively religious, and absolutely true to her decent instincts. Listening to her is an enormous pleasure." —Doris Grumbach

"Boyd writes with good sense, power and grace." —*Richmond News Leader*

"It takes a Southerner to truly understand and appreciate sin. We were probably the first Americans to say, 'Lead us not into temptation. We can find it ourselves.' Blanche Boyd in *The Redneck Way of Knowledge* followed her temptations. . . . Knowing that Jesus died for her sins, Blanche sinned continuously so that his sacrifice wouldn't be wasted. . . . [Her] philosophy seems marvelously sane. . . . Her insights vibrate with originality." —Rita Mae Brown, *Washington Post Book World*

"Bright, appealing personal essays . . . both funny and serious, written in a voice very much her own." —*Publishers Weekly*

Blanche McCrary Boyd
The Redneck
Way of Knowledge

Blanche McCrary Boyd is the author of *The Revolution of Little Girls* and two earlier novels. Her articles and short stories have appeared in *The Village Voice*, *Esquire*, *Rolling Stone*, and *Playboy*. She grew up in Charleston, South Carolina, and now lives in Connecticut, where she teaches writing at Connecticut College. Ms. Boyd is currently at work on a new novel.

The Redneck
Way of Knowledge

DOWN-HOME TALES

Blanche McCrary Boyd

VINTAGE CONTEMPORARIES
Vintage Books
A Division of Random House, Inc.
New York

FIRST VINTAGE BOOK EDITION, JANUARY 1995

The pieces of this book were originally published in slightly different
form in *The Village Voice*.

The Library of Congress has cataloged the Knopf edition as follows:
Boyd, Blanche M. [date]
The redneck way of knowledge.
Contents: Aunt Jenny at the Rockettes—The redneck
way of knowledge—Be here then—A thousand words
about a picture—John Paul's passion play—[etc.]
I. Title.
PS3552.08775R4   823'.54   81–48138
ISBN 0-394-51050-X   AACR2

Vintage ISBN: 0-679-75767-8

AUTHOR'S NOTE

To protect friends and relatives from my indiscretions, I have often
disguised personalities, altered encounters, and changed names.
Characters identified by first names only are usually "fictionalized"
in this way; characters identified by full names are real and have
been rendered as accurately as possible.

Manufactured in the United States of America
10 9 8 7 6 5 4 3 2 1

This book is for my mother, Mildred McCrary Corbin, who kept asking why I didn't write books people would understand, and for my sister, Patricia McCrary-Smith, who never questioned me about anything. I offer them my deepest love and thought.

CONTENTS

INTRODUCTION TO THE VINTAGE EDITION

I met Blanche Boyd for the first time almost twenty years ago at Sagaris, a Feminist institute that she had helped to organize. I was there with two other members of my lesbian-feminist collective, soaking up Yankee wisdom and flirting with revolutionary fervor. Back then I was much younger and more terrified of the world's opinions, but working hard not to show that fear. At the time, Blanche looked pretty fearless and her first novel, *Nerves*, was continuing to garner admiration. She seemed to me to be very soft-spoken for a successful published author. I didn't know enough to guess that she was supporting herself writing indexes for other people's books, that being successful meant even more pressure and more uncertainty. At the time, I was not really writing, just thinking about writing. Actually publishing anything was a great unknown, and I was hesitant to ask too many questions of someone who had done what I only dreamed of doing.

Close to a decade later, *The Redneck Way of Knowledge* was published, and a lot had changed for both Blanche and me. She had published another novel and moved back down South, along the way developing a reputation for these insightful and highly personal pieces that had been appearing in the *Village Voice*. I was living in New York City, editing a magazine, and just starting to publish my own stories, clipping Blanche's stories to show friends. The book saved me a lot of trouble. Finally I could easily show people what I had been talking about—this Southern girl who was writing these marvelous human portraits that weren't really journalism but something more. I acquired three copies of that book in a week—two that were given to me and one I paid for in hardcover. I picked up a couple more at used book stores in the next two years. By stubborn attention to who was allowed to borrow the book, I still had four copies when I left New York for California in 1987. But six years of teaching and loaning books to friends slowly robbed me of those extra copies. It was my fault. I was always quoting one bit or another, making my students read "Be Here Then" for a succinct explication of how storytelling works on the page, how stories stretch, exaggerate, make larger than life. How in fiction "the past tense reads as if it were the present while the present tense acquires a dreamlike feeling." The mark of a truly great writer, I would tell my students, is to introduce you to a figure of fun and then make you care about them. Read this, I would say, read about her friend Dixie and see what I mean. Then I would get indignant and tell them that, no, the book wasn't in print any more. I shouldn't have been surprised, I suppose, when my copies kept disappearing.

When Blanche's novel *The Revolution of Little Girls* was published in 1991, I met up with her again. I was finishing my novel, *Bastard Out of Carolina*, and I was also years past my fear of offending. I set up an interview with Blanche just to get a chance to talk to her again. Once we'd caught up a bit, I asked her when there was going to be another edition of *Redneck*.

"I only got one copy of that book left," I said to her. "And it's the one with all my notes. I need about five new copies that I can pass around." Blanche stared at me for a moment and then admitted that she was thinking about the book again.

I tried to explain to her how much I loved the book, how much I had used it, and how much it had helped me as I was dealing with the same issues the book treats so carefully: the long process of reclaiming your heritage while rejecting the prejudices and hatreds everyone else seems to think come with the territory. Blanche started to smile, very slowly, as if she wasn't sure she believed me. "You really think *Redneck*'s that good?" she asked me.

"Honey," I said very carefully. "I think it's a cultural masterpiece."

Rereading *Redneck* now, I am reminded every time of how much alike and how different Blanche Boyd and I are. Both of us are lesbians, Southerners, expatriate writers, prickly and rebellious at being labeled any one thing too firmly. Both of us are completely conscious of all the ways our family and region have shaped our approach to the world—rebels with a cause, you might say, clinging stubbornly to whal we have loved, even as we work hard to make clear all that needs to change. It is that quality that is so precious and surprising. Blanche Boyd's essays recognize the inherent strengths and wisdom that are found in the wounded people we have loved so much and with whom we have sometimes been so angry—their separate and distinct perception of the life we have lived together.

Redneck's the book I have loaned other runaways who seemed to me as lost as I was. It has been the book I quoted when I needed to explain how deep and painful family connections can be, how history presses down on us—personal as well as social history. Over and over again I have had people come back to me and say, yes, this is how it is. You go home and you find yourself again.

As a girl, I too knew my family was not normal, and like Blanche, I was jealous of Yankees who had both snow and basements. I watched late-night television and dreamed of growing up to be sophisticated, witty, a woman capable of the devastating one-liners Blanche sprinkles through her essays like sugar on a Krispy Kreme donut. And fearless, oh yes, I wanted to be fearless—the kind of fearless that could afford to tell the truth about our fears and aspirations. The absolute own-your-own approach to racism, class contempt, and family bigotry that Blanche displays is exactly what I wanted to grow up to achieve. Truth is, I wanted to grow up to be Blanche Boyd—the Blanche Boyd who wrote *Redneck* and claimed her life as fearlessly as a heroine in a country-western song.

But what exactly is the redneck way of knowledge, I have been asked. A stance, I would say. More than a decade ago I learned in karate classes that the secret to survival was stance, your feet planted firmly and your weight centered so you could move as you want without risk of tripping yourself up. It sounds easy, like dancing should be, but a good stance requires that attention be paid to the self in a way we do not normally assume. You have to learn what is normal for you and then know how to change it. Why do I lead with my chin, my head thrust determinedly forward as if my whole body were in flight? What am I fleeing or running toward?

Having been born in a region more mythical than examined, I am Southern to the core and have always known myself and my people— not only hicks but rednecks, noted for walking and talking slow, except under the impetus of chemicals or outrage. A people washed in the water of guilt and resentment, the blood of Sweet Jesus and the liquor of Pentecostal possession. My particular generation has hated itself for being white and racist, and still has hummed along to Lynyrd Skynyrd with authentic rebel righteousness. Our stance is perplexed. For those of us who have survived, that curious need to understand has become a source of strength—of stability in a rocky world. Feet planted firmly among those who raised us, we tilt our chins back to observe where we came from, go home and acknowledge our common origin. We do it almost religiously. As Blanche says about her family in the first of these pieces, "We all know where we stand, and we don't discuss our differences. I eat their delicious food, admire their eccentricities, and love them with the same complexity with which I once despised them."

Redneck demonstrates the power of authentic voice, the essential necessity of truth-telling, and the power of mining your own life and experience for powerful revelation. What I have loved about this book is how the author goes naked in it, shows us her fears, passions, prejudices, and small moments as stubbornly as she shows us the people she is writing about, the self-exposure justifying the revelations she makes about people. As each piece rolls out, we learn more and more about what it feels like to grow up in the South, leave, and come home again ready to see people for who they really are. Blanche seems to feel no need to pillory anyone or reduce them to mawkish romanticized cartoons. This is simply great story-telling, and it captures a slice of the South the way James Baldwin could—though Blanche first makes you laugh where Baldwin makes you cry. Both bring you insight and revelation, the authentic rebel perspective.

The redneck way of knowledge is intrinsically strengthened by humor. A sense of irony and the absurd is at the core of Blanche's work, as it is in the writing of Randall Kenan, Allan Gurganus, Fannie Flagg, Rita Mae Brown, and, yes, in my own work. We know who we are but we're still trying to talk it all out. We are the people who can say that nothing is more important than the ones you love, that our central allegiance has to be to our families. Then, we all might add, "Fuck all that." Slow respect and rueful laughter.

It is contrast that teaches us so much about ourselves. One of the things I share with Blanche Boyd is the experience of moving north and learning about myself and my culture by observing how I did and did not fit in with Yankees. The contrast defines us: mildly barbaric, a little too earthy, profoundly sexual, living in the moment as easily as the past, and alienated from family and region, not only by political convictions but by a rude sense of embarrassment, a self-consciousness about the less admirable intransigences of our heritage—that rock-bound prejudice that seriously undermines sanity and the intellect.

No Southerner is ever unconscious about race and class, and we know it. Encountering Yankees who blithely insisted they never noticed their black friends were black, I thought it first some very subtle joke, and then a completely revealing cultural myth. Who did they think they were kidding? You should read Blanche Boyd, I would tell them. Get some perspective. You Southerners think everyone is like you, I was told. Uh huh. I do.

Yankee knowledge might also be redneck. I've run into that a time or two. There is a funky transcendence as bitterly evident in the concrete reaches of Manhattan as the maple-scented quarries of Vermont. Just as racist and class-bound as the South, but sure of its worth and full of caustic humor. It's the self-reflecting humor I like, the kind of droll twang that once stopped me in a bookstore to demand, "Why is it all you Southerners have so many cousins?"

"Well," I replied. "We just keep track of ours. And what I don't understand is how come you don't."

Family then. Blanche Boyd tells us down-home redneck truths about family and the wisdom to be found in grating your own nerves against those of the ones you both love and despise. I recognize it as a redneck variation on a Zen insight. It's a truth people could barely stand to hear a decade ago, and I suspect it is only a little more acceptable now. But it is the essential thing, the part of the redneck stance that must be felt from the inside—pain and great love, shame and enormous enjoyment. All are products of looking closely at your family, nation, and people. When Blanche Boyd looks to her own. I see my people and love them all over again. Never mind that the McCrary kin would have despised the Gibsons, the Gibsons hated the McCrarys. We are our families and something new as well. That's the redneck way of knowledge.

Here are stubbornly revealing portraits of individuals you may not recognize, but who are so much a part of the landscape in which I grew up I have to smile every time I read them over. More importantly, this is an enormously affectionate and wise book, brimming over with compassion for a people and place too often approached with contempt. Blanche does that complicated thing, she does not abandon her family or renounce her love for them. She bluntly refuses to adopt their more problematic hatred and shameful secrets but she clings to them none-theless, seeing her life reflected in theirs.

This is the purest sort of love, a love that sees the beloved whole and hangs in anyway. The strongest knowledge we can share, the deep knowledge of complete self-acceptance. Yankee or Southerner, queer or so-called normal, you can find yourself in this book, and know yourself loved.

These days Blanche Boyd lives off the green coast of Connecticut, drives a teenage muscle car—a Firebird formula—wears dark shades, short hair, loose black shirts over the muscles of a swimmer's body, and great cowboy boots, all in all the perfect image of an expatriate female Southern troublemaker. One might imagine that image has nothing to do with reality but us 'necks know better. Sometimes presentation of self is all we can control, and seeing ourselves as actors in the movie of our lives—characters in the story—is all too tempting. These tales were written not in the pursuit of gonzo journalism but in a more deliberate approach, essentially redneck—which is to say a risk-taking, wise-cracking, passionately engaged writer's approach. And whether taking her aunt to visit the Rockettes, riding out a hurricane, or following the Pope's travels, Blanche Boyd brings insight, amusement and great passion to an old custom—revealing the new by talking out the old.

Dorothy Allison
September 1994

Aunt Jenny
at the Rockettes

Last winter I telephoned my Aunt Jenny for the first time in eighteen years. "You probably don't remember me, Aunt Jenny," I said. "This is Mack's daughter Blanche."

"Why, Blanche," she said, as if it had only been a few weeks since she'd heard from me, "we'd been wondering when you would call."

Aunt Jenny is the matriarch of my daddy's side of our family, in the Upcountry of South Carolina. Our branch of the family lives in the Lowcountry, in Charleston. When I was thirteen, my father was killed in an accident. His funeral had been my last contact with Aunt Jenny.

When her geriatric group toured New York City, Aunt Jenny skipped the Greyhound ride to West Point and spent the day with me. We talked for six hours in the lobby of the Taft Hotel. Jenny had been amused to think I might not recognize her; she claimed she could identify our family type whether she knew the individual or not.

I wasn't sure what had awakened such a hunger, but I sat deeply attentive while Aunt Jenny told me stories about my kin. She gave me a photograph, a portrait of my great-grandparents and their six children; my grandmother, whom I'm named for, stared out at me as a solemn ten-year-old.

I didn't see Aunt Jenny again for quite a while. Then, two months ago, she phoned me urgently. She needed three tickets to go see the Rockettes on Good Friday. Radio City Music Hall was going to close, this was to be the last Easter show, and she wanted her two granddaughters to see it. Jenny had heard from a member of her touring group that tickets were going fast, and she insisted I rush to the box office. Naturally, she hoped I would join them for the show. I said I'd get the tickets, but I didn't want to see the Rockettes. No, I admitted, I never had. Aunt Jenny said the Rockettes were history, and I should think it over.

I thought it over.

My other chance to see the Rockettes had been on my high school senior trip. To earn money, our class sold Krispy Kreme doughnuts every Friday afternoon, and after ball games we held dances in the lunchroom. After graduation, we boarded a chartered Greyhound for five crammed days: two in Washington, D.C. (I climbed the Washington Monument); a brief stopover in Luray Caverns, Virginia; and three days in New York City.

We stayed at the Taft Hotel. The street was lined with buses chartered from high schools all over the country. The Taft was like a high school convention. I was sixteen years old, and breathless with the thrill of being in New York City. My dream was to grow up and live there.

I started wanting to leave the South when I was eight years old and we got a television. We got our set before the

Charleston station actually opened, so I spent long hours staring at the test pattern of the station's logo—an American Indian in a headdress with the channel numbers written on his headband. I was suspicious about the outside world, and I was waiting for television to give me the word.

I saw movies almost every night at the drive-in (that's how our neighborhood's parents entertained their children), but I did not connect the people in the movies with anything I knew. Maybe it was because the screen was so large. But the people on television were little, and they were more ordinary, too. When the logo disappeared and television programs appeared in its place, a dreadful truth came clear to me: Southerners were not normal people. We did not sound like normal people, or have the same style of physical movement. What we chose to talk about seemed peculiarly different also. I began to realize we were hicks.

It was a lot for an eight-year-old to deal with; I was already suspicious because of basements and snow. We didn't have any snow in South Carolina, and in school the textbooks showed beautiful pictures of neighborhoods covered with icing. And I knew normal houses had basements. Even the houses in the Dick and Jane books had basements. But, since Charleston was at sea level and was ocean-bottom flat, houses were flush with the ground. I dreamed of having a secret room under the house, a place for dark, warm choices no one else would know about.

Television confirmed my suspicions and took away my faith in my surroundings. I didn't want to be a hick. I decided to go North, where people talked fast, walked fast, had basements, wrote books, and acted cool. I practiced talking like the people on television. Sometimes I imagined that I could step into the screen and reappear in New York City.

After my father's death, I became desperate to leave the South. I talked loud to intensify my courage. My family was no longer a source of connection for me but an octopus that squirmed across the state. My rebellion brought out their values as nakedly as it exposed my fear. My mother and aunts and uncles and cousins made it clear that nothing I wanted, nothing about me, mattered as much as the family did. A child was the raw material for the family; the adults' task was to form that child properly; the goal was the survival, endurance, growth, and prosperity of the tribe. If I chose to leave, it was a condemned decision. I was expendable, of course, but a traitor.

By the time of my senior trip, selling Krispy Kreme doughnuts every Friday was a form of yoga. The snake shivering up my spine was New York City. When we got to New York, I realized the Taft Hotel was not the best, so I pretended I was staying at the Americana. I stayed up all night in the coffeeshop in the lobby, because I had never seen a shop that stayed open all night. I went to the top of the Empire State Building and tried to look like a real New Yorker. I ate a bagel. I imagined getting mugged. I practiced feeling glamorous and damned. It was great. The only thing my tour group saw that I missed was Radio City Music Hall and the Rockettes.

I wasn't sure what Radio City Music Hall was, but I pictured it vaguely as either looking like the interior of a very large radio or as having walls that were covered with radios. I knew the Rockettes were a group who wore bathing-suit-type outfits and kicked in unison, like majorettes at a football game. With the instinct of the kid born to leave home, I knew the Rockettes were, as I would have said then, *hicksville*. I skipped the Rockettes, had a steak dinner at Tad's, and went to the theatre to see *Camelot*.

When I was eighteen I left the South with a pose of ferocious finality. I was afraid that if I let down my angry mask for a moment I would be swept back, and my family's smothering abuse would seduce me.

I got married, soon moved to California, and tried to get educated. I refused to watch television and began to exorcise my accent. It didn't work. Almost every summer I returned to the wide, flat marshes of the Lowcountry with a lump of homesickness in my throat. I fought viciously and often with my mother, the Lowcountry branch matriarch. But, as my identity away from home became more established, I became less afraid of how much I cared about them. When I got divorced seven years later, they were mildly hopeful I would move back home. Instead, I moved to New York City.

Being a white Southerner is a bit like being Eichmann's daughter: People don't assume you're guilty, but they wonder how you've been affected. My family is ideologically upfront right wing. I never met a liberal until I went away to college. A vulnerable relative was quickly institutionalized for being homosexual. When I became involved in radical politics in the late sixties, it was the equivalent, for my family, of becoming a criminal.

We all mellowed in the seventies, or gave up on each other, depending on how you want to look at it. Recently, when a woman lover and I broke up after five years, my mother called to console me. "You must feel terrible," she said, "just like when you got divorced." Last summer when my sister married a man in charge of firing missiles from Polaris submarines, I was in the wedding. We all know where we stand, and we don't discuss our differences. I eat their delicious food, admire their eccentricities, and love them with the same complexity with which I once despised them.

I called Aunt Jenny back. It was true, I was dying to see the Rockettes on Good Friday with two cousins I hadn't met.

· · ·

The auditorium of Radio City Music Hall looks like a stylized sunrise. There is a huge proscenium arch, and the walls and ceilings are formed by more arches. It's like being inside an inverted gold bowl.

I kept thinking of halos.

When the orchestra rose from the pit, bathed in a pale blue light, I experienced the same sexual elation I had felt as a teenager watching *Camelot*. There were so many forbidden flashbulbs it seemed as if strobe lights were part of the show.

Since it was the Easter special, many religious motifs were exploited. There was a church scene with the Rockettes in something resembling nuns' habits, only the headpieces were tall and double-pointed, medieval in effect. After the nunlike figures formed a cross under the stained-glass windows of the backdrop, the curtain fell. It was like a parody of *The Seventh Seal*.

The orchestra played a medley of nonmusic, and Mr. Joe McGrath sang "Easter Parade" standing in front of a backdrop that looked like a Whitman's Sampler box. Next came the Bunny Frolics. Not *Playboy* bunnies, but baggy-assed terrycloth, pastel bunnies with ears and masks and tails. I began to get horrified.

The bunnies pretended they were ladies and compared hats. Two bunnies soft-shoed "Give me that old soft shoe." Then there were the bunny romances: "Sweetheart, will you love me forever?" A gold lamé bunny sang, "I got a right to sing the blues." Three frumpy bunnies in polka-dot skirts sang a jazzed-up version of "A Tisket, a Tasket." There was even an Elvis bunny singing "Hound Dog." I began to get a headache. Aunt Jenny was chortling. I wanted to stand up on the first mezzanine and yell something obscene.

Instead, I went to get popcorn. When I came back, I saw that Aunt Jenny was so tiny that her feet were resting toes-only on the floor. She was wearing a blue raincoat. She and my cousins, who looked like guppies under water, were rapt and happy. I settled down.

When the Rockettes came onto the great stage, they seemed as exotic as violence. They wore plumed headdresses and silver costumes. Their precision was absolute. Big Easter eggs around the sides of the gold hall lit up while the Rockettes marched and kicked. When they filed in front of the orchestra and high-stepped, the audience went wild. Flashbulbs popped everywhere.

Afterward, my cousins seemed disappointed. "Is that all?" one of them asked. It wasn't all. We stayed for *Crossed Swords*, a movie version of Mark Twain's *The Prince and the Pauper*, starring just about everybody. Then we went to dinner around the corner at Joe's Pier 52.

On the street, Aunt Jenny clung to my arm. She has wisely, in our encounters, avoided asking personal questions, and she has not read either of the novels I've written about South Carolina. But on the street, walking to Joe's Pier 52, she remarked, "I'd like to get a vacuum cleaner and clean out your mind."

I burst out laughing. Aunt Jenny tried to look stern while we waited for a light to change. It was too cold for what she and my cousins were wearing, and Jenny's eyes were watery. "I view your life as a tragedy, Blanche," she said.

I peered into her face to see if she was serious. "How can it be a tragedy if I'm doing what I want?"

She smiled, showing me she understood our conflicts to their depths. "I guess that's the problem, isn't it."

I am trying to sort through the good ways my family and being a Southerner have affected me, and separate out the destructive influences. It's not easy. Since my lover and I ended our relationship, my grief has been more difficult to deal with than I expected. I tell myself frenzied jokes.

Breakin' up is hard to do, I've been broken-hearted all broke up falling to pieces over you. I tried to put it all back together and it looked like Frankenstein's monster. I know these are images of disintegration. At times I feel as if the pieces of my psychic makeup have broken off from each other in chunks.

I am mourning a personal loss, but I am also mourning my family's myth about me. Their fairy tale is that I'll meet a man or a woman (this scenario is apparently adjustable to any situation) and fall in love and live happily ever after. I'll "get over this phase," "see the light," and stop being so guiltily loyal to my work. I'll see that nothing is more important than the ones you love, that my central allegiance has to be to my family. Luckily, there's another stone chunk of me around to say, *Fuck all that.*

My family sent a thin filament far into my psyche, like the webbed roots of grass spreading under a sidewalk. Years after I thought they could affect me so deeply, the roots of their beliefs pushed upward and cracked my life apart.

I want to make peace with my inheritance, and my family seems to want to incorporate me at any cost. At dinner Aunt Jenny says, "Tell the girls about all those demonstrations, Blanche. About the war and all. Tell them about when you were arrested." I feel our similar blood, sitting in Joe's Pier 52, while my young cousins, their fried shrimps clutched solemnly in midair, listen to my stories of the sixties. Aunt Jenny informs me that my hatred of celery is inherited. Uncle Willis felt the same way.

Like most clichés, Aunt Jenny and the Rockettes have an honorable history, and I have learned a slow respect. I went to see the Rockettes for the same reason I go back to South Carolina every summer, for the same reason I watch television. I cried my way through *Crossed Swords* for the same reason I cry when I hear "Dixie": These values are built into my character, like the way I hold my shoulders.

Aunt Jenny tells me this trip to New York is her last. She calls it her swan song. It's true she signs off yearly, but it's also true that she's old, and maybe this time she's right. Aunt Jenny and the Rockettes are dying forms; I'm grateful I learned to see them. Aunt Jenny says it doesn't matter about the folding of the Rockettes. Nowadays, she says, you can see a better show anytime you want to, on television, at halftime for the Dallas Cowboys.

The Redneck
Way of Knowledge

When I was living in California and still trying to pass as a hip suburban housewife, I got interested in Esalen. I was a graduate student at Stanford, and since Esalen held special weekend workshops right on campus, it was easy to attend some sessions. The first one I went to was an introduction to sensitivity training. In this Esalen buffet, I sampled yoga, screaming, sticking my fingers down my throat without gagging, spinal awareness, and falling down.

The facilitator said that adults, especially American adults, are afraid of falling down. Look how easily kids fall down and recover. Being afraid to fall down makes you stiff. It makes you afraid of risks in general. So we went outside on the grass in front of the Stanford library, the instructor said, "*Fall!*" and we all flopped down in simulated spontaneity. We did this over and over. I was hoping that nobody I knew would see me behaving like this. Of course, in my acting class I'd already had to study a raccoon and spend half an hour crawling around the fountain in front of the bookstore, getting in touch with the raccoon in me; when I found myself rolling around the Stanford lawn with a group of adults who seemed otherwise unremarkable, I was not totally unprepared.

In the second workshop I went to, we did kundalini yoga under self-hypnosis. I already knew something about hypnosis. When I was a teenager I taught myself to hypnotize other people. "Look only at the tip of my cigarette, your eyelids are getting heavy," I said to a young cousin. I kept saying that kind of thing, and then I counted slowly to ten. She went into a trance. I reversed the procedure and she came out of it. Soon I learned to hypnotize willing people with regular success. When I first went to college, I used to do hypnosis as a party trick. At Duke, women were still required to wear skirts, had to be in the dorms by midnight, and were forbidden to smoke cigarettes standing up; they made a new rule about hypnosis by students. Eventually I was asked to leave the Harvard of the South, but before I left I volunteered as a subject at the Parapsychology Laboratory there. At the Parapsychology Lab I was taught self-hypnosis. "Deep body relaxation," Dr. La called it, but I knew better. After a few sessions I could put myself in a trance as easily as I could put others into one.

The kundalini workshop was called "Psychedelic Experiences Through Hypnosis." One reason I took it was that I wanted to have an acid experience without the risk of taking acid. I had left my hypnosis experiments behind because once in a self-induced trance I hallucinated that my arm was ballooning out and I was breathing through my elbow. This experience scared me, but it didn't seem as potentially frightening as LSD. I thought a psychedelic experience through hypnosis would be a good mockup.

The workshop leader taught self-hypnosis and I quickly relocated my ability to go into trances. Then the leader explained the basic theory of kundalini yoga. In kundalini, he said, we conceive of a snake wrapped around the base of the spine. We try to raise this snake up the spine to the top of the head, where it mates with Siva and we reach ecstatic enlightenment. There are seven stages of raising this snake, and seven corresponding places on the spine. Kundalini chants are designed to make each place, or cakra, on the spine vibrate. After chanting all evening Friday and all day Saturday, when I returned on Sunday my mind was enervated. I kept slipping into an eyes-open state that was much like being unconscious. We began to chant again. My legs went to sleep. The instructor told me to lie down on my back. The energy rising through my body, he said, had rendered my legs temporarily useless. As we chanted, I could feel each of the cakras on my spine vibrating. I could feel that snake sliding up. The leader had told us that sometimes the energy gets trapped in the neck and causes headaches. Since I am extremely suggestible, when the snake reached my neck I developed a pulsing flashing pain in the back of my skull. The leader touched my neck for a few minutes and the pain disappeared. We reached the last cakra, and after three days of chanting, there was finally silence. The leader said Om, and I felt as if two hinged flaps on the top of my head opened upward. A white light poured out. The release was unexpected and surprisingly gentle. My mind felt like a countertop that had been wiped clean. For several days I initiated no conversations, and when spoken to, I would sometimes forget to reply.

Noise and falling, scientists say, are the only fears we're born with; all our others are learned, acquired. Maybe my choice of Esalen workshops indicated a personality pattern, because, in the past four months, since I have returned to live in the town where I grew up, I have developed two new interests: skydiving and stock-car racing. Falling and noise.

. . .

I left South Carolina fifteen years ago, as if it were a burning building. I have returned cautiously, deliberately. What does it mean to love a place? I was grown before I found out Roosevelt didn't cause the Depression; I had lived in the North several years before someone suggested to me that to love the song "Dixie" was racist in itself. In the North I always felt mildly barbaric, a little too earthy, and I worried that I drank too much.

Recently a New York friend came to visit me here in Charleston. We went to a Rites of Spring party on a magnificent plantation on the Ashley River. In the evening there was an oyster roast in a grove of dogwoods, camellias, azaleas. Two young women began to wrestle on the ground and everyone gathered around them chanting, "Rut, rut, rut." My friend said, "I never saw anything quite like it."

Maybe it's the heat, maybe it's the sweat, maybe it's the constant sexual smell of the ocean, but the Puritans didn't have much impact on the South Carolina Lowcountry. The young woman who owns the plantation lived in California for a couple of years, but she got tired of it. "Everybody was always trying to be so laidback. They were always trying to relax, and they tried so *hard*. They don't drink much either. It made me nervous." We were riding around drinking white wine we kept iced down in a cooler. Drinking is a serious pastime here, and so is riding around. When you leave someone's house, it's not uncommon for them to offer you a "traveler," a drink in a paper cup to nurse you to your next destination. I keep a flask in my glove compartment. *Be Here Now* was a radical notion when I was living in California, but the Southerners I have come home to would be bewildered by such advice. Where else would they be? They talk plainer and call the seductions of the moment "having a good time."

Falling and noise. We fall in love, we fall in debt, we fall in with each other, fall out, fall behind, over, ill, short, in battle. We fall from grace. Our faces fall. Our arches fall. It was silly to think I could confront my fear of falling by flopping around on the Stanford lawn. Here in South Carolina, where my past is all around me, I am becoming a connoisseur of the present. I step out of airplanes.

A magazine editor gave me an assignment to learn skydiving. I did it for the money and the dare. I continued it for the thrills. I've jumped more than a dozen times now. Each time the jump master opens the plane door and I climb out onto the wing in an eighty-mile-an-hour wind, each time I experience the purity of freefall, I am so wired I feel luminous. The skydiver falls belly-first, arms and legs stretched back in an ecstatic position. Stepping out of a plane is not like stepping off a roof. The human body does not believe it can fall thousands of feet and survive, but the mind devises a method. In this collision of mind and instinct are moments that are like holes torn in the world. I feel as if I step through them to somewhere else. In freefall, as in orgasm, the conscious mind shrinks in the face of an astounding animal rush. In California a lot of us were talking about altered states. I'm still talking about altered states, but now I want them raw, like oysters.

I went to the Darlington 500 because I thought it would be better than kundalini yoga under hypnosis. To get ready for Darlington, I went to the Summerville Speedway. The Summerville Speedway is a dirt track, a reddish quarter-mile oval where local boys and local garages compete. Sometimes more important races, like a qualifier for the Sundrop 100, are held here, but mostly this is a neighborhood affair. During the season three classes of races are held every Saturday night. Families come carrying coolers and cushions and kids. It was at Summerville, with my chest rumbling and red dust in my nostrils, that I began to understand racing.

I had smoked a joint in the car. The noise didn't feel so overwhelming at first. During the time trials, only one car was on the track at any given moment. I drank a couple of beers and ate some boiled peanuts. Down in front of the bleachers a gang of kids played peaceably in the loose dirt. Their toys were about fifty crushed beer cans. "REDNECK MONTESSORI!" I screamed at my companion.

I screamed because the race had begun. I had never experienced noise and speed straight up before, like bourbon. My chest cavity was vibrating. So were the bleachers. I began to feel oddly happy. "IT'S LIKE A RAMONES CONCERT WITHOUT THE MUSIC!"

There was a twelve-car wreck. "YAAAAAAYYYYYYY," sang the kids in front of the bleachers. We scrambled down to watch the tow trucks untangle the cars. No one was hurt. "This is nothing!" my friend said. "Wait till you get to Darlington!"

Stock-car racing is a redneck sport. It originated among moonshine runners who souped up their cars so they could escape the feds. (Remember Robert Mitchum in *Thunder Road*?) For fun they tested their driving skills and hand-modified cars against each other. Now dirt tracks are scattered through other parts of the country, and there are a few big speedways in California, Michigan, and Delaware, but stock-car racing has remained primarily a Southern phenomenon. The most important speedways are in Daytona, Darlington, Charlotte, Talladega. These asphalt ovals range in length from a mile and a quarter at Darlington to 2.67 miles at Talladega. The track at Talladega is banked so steeply it would be difficult to walk on the curves. On the big tracks, speeds can go over two hundred miles an hour. Windshields can cave in at speeds like that. Pit crews are so efficient they can change two tires and gas up a car in 13 seconds. They can replace a blown engine in 13 minutes. The metal bodies of these cars are sanded almost paper thin; then the weight that would have been in the hull is redistributed with pieces of lead, to help the car hold the road better.

Going to one of the major races is an event you have to plan for: A remarkable survey at one of the Darlington races revealed that more than three-fourths of the fans had bought their tickets at least a month in advance. This remarkable survey also revealed that 40 percent of the fans drank Anheuser Busch Natural Light beer. Thirty-two percent drank Miller Lite. Coke was favored over Pepsi, and country music was better than any other kind. Twenty-three percent smoked Winstons. One quarter had bought Goodyear tires within the last year. Half used Champion sparkplugs. A quarter used Purolator filters. More than a third cranked up in the morning with Die-Hard batteries. In stock-car racing, as in the Old West, brands matter.

At Darlington, for a Sunday race, fans begin to arrive on Thursday, when the time trials are held. In the trials, each driver is allowed two laps to qualify. The fastest cars get the best starting positions. On Friday, more fans straggle in. They settle down for the weekend in the parking lot, or they pay $15 extra and park in the infield. Some bring platforms to put on top of their campers. On the platforms they have a good view; they can sunbathe, drink beer, and otherwise feel above it all. Friday night is mildly festive. Cookouts make the air fragrant. There is some drinking, but mostly people are holding out to do their serious partying on Saturday.

On Saturday campers and cars and pickups and vans and even tractor-trailers pour into the infield and the parking lots. The grass disappears. Rednecks pile out of their vehicles. Of course, not everyone at Darlington is working class, and not everyone is white. I did spot four blacks, and, among the 65,000 people attending, I'm sure there were a few others. But mostly these are good ole boys and good ole gals. These folks are real comfortable with that Confederate flag flying over the Speedway. They have decals on their cars and clothes identifying their racing heroes. I saw Darrell Waltrip fans, Buddy Baker fans, Richard Petty fans, Cale Yarborough fans, Dale Earnhardt fans, and fans of both the Allison brothers, Bobby and Donnie. Popular among racing fans are lightweight nylon jackets with patches sewn on them. The patches say the names of races and speedways—"Charlotte International Speedway," "Daytona Firecracker 400," "World 600"— but they also say things like "First National City Traveler's Checks" and "Coburg Dairy."

I went to the Rebel 500 in a camper with two chief petty officers, a Summerville policeman, and their wives. My sister is married to one of the chiefs. Patty had packed barbecued spareribs, boiled peanuts, and deviled eggs. Another of the wives had fried chicken. In our coolers were more than a dozen beers for each person. I popped my first Natural Light at 9 a.m., and by the time we arrived at Darlington at noon, I had a nice buzz going.

It was a gray day. We found our seats on the fourth turn and settled in. I felt a little bored, but the people I was with were already excited. Roger, my brother-in-law, grabbed my arm. "Just wait," he said. "When they say, 'Gentlemen, start your engines,' you won't believe it. The *noise.*"

I waited. "Miss Winston" was introduced, "one of the world's most beautiful girls." Then another of the world's most beautiful girls was introduced. Then came the "visiting pacesetter cars," two *Star Wars*–inspired automobiles named Galaxy II and Death Ship II. Galaxy II and Death Ship II are both capable of driving faster than the record speeds at

Darlington. They rear up on their tails and scoot along. They look like rockets. Unfortunately, one of them, to quote the announcer, "didn't get it up," and the forces of death prevailed. The pacesetter cars were accompanied by *Star Wars* characters: one guy in white fur, one in black armor, and two young women wearing black bathing suits with silver trim. Apparently women, to be out of this world, don't need as many modifications as men do.

After the *Star Wars* fizzle, the fan club buses paraded by. Then came the parade of tow trucks. Eight of them. I ate a piece of chicken and popped my fifth beer. I was not so much bored now as bewildered. "Why did they bring the tow trucks by?" I asked. No one answered.

It was time for the invocation. The preacher entreated the heavenly father to take the drivers into a new manhood. He talked a long time. Someone in front of me whispered, "He should shut up." Near the end, the preacher said, "May the best *car*—and the best *man*—*win!*"

A lot of people were wearing earmuffs. I asked Roger about them. "They're radios," he said. "If you listen to the race at the same time you watch it, you know quicker what's happening. If there's an accident on the backstretch or something."

A worn tape of the National Anthem played over the P.A. system. Then the announcer said, "*And now . . . for the most dramatic moment in the world of sports . . . Gentlemen, start your engines!*"

A roar went up from the stands. Behind it was the sharper roar of the cars. The noise was intense, but not what I had prepared for. I was disappointed. Maybe it was because we were high in the stands. Maybe stock-car racing just wasn't as thrilling as skydiving. I'd jumped twice the day before, and maybe I'd taken my edge off. Maybe I just liked dirt-track racing better.

The race started. Soon the noise was relentless, enveloping. It wore away at everything. I watched the fans watch the race. They seemed familiar with every car and driver. They screamed and cheered.

"Pick somebody to root for!" Roger yelled. "You'll have a better time!" Roger's man was Richard Petty, King Richard, No. 43, Mr. STP. I didn't really care who won.

It takes about thirty seconds to run a lap. A 500-mile race at Darlington is 367 laps. With caution flags slowing the action, a race lasts about three hours. I settled in.

After fifty laps my eyes got tired. The cars seemed to come around the track faster and faster while the track got smaller and smaller. The great whine of engines became rhythmical. My eyelids were getting heavy. I tried to concentrate on the gray breeze blowing, on the smell of burned rubber, on smoke drifting from barbecues in the infield. I watched a hefty blonde sunbathing on top of a camper.

One hundred laps. Petty and Waltrip were fighting for the lead. Yarborough was trying to keep up. So was Earnhardt.

My neck ached. I was a whole chorus of inner distractions now, little bladelike pains, grainy eyes, the heaviness of sleep.

"Pit stop!" I yelled at my sister and made my way down the long concrete steps, out of the stands. The bathrooms were under the bleachers. Beer cans and other debris clunked onto the roof like a huge metallic rain. It was funny. I felt better.

When I was back in my seat I ate some chicken. My mind cleared. I began to cheer for Richard Petty. Yarborough had been lapped. "That'll teach that turkey farmer," my sister said. Petty was in the lead. "King Richard," she said, "is definitely the coolest."

A dozen state troopers marched up our aisle. They climbed to the top row and settled in to watch the race. They wore heavy leather boots, gun belts, sunglasses, cowboy hats. The term "state trooper" is much more frightening than "highway patrolman." George Wallace's boys taught me that. One of the troopers was speaking with fatherly benevolence to a fidgety boy who had been throwing beer cans at the people walking below the bleachers.

My head pounded. I wadded up pieces of toilet paper and stuffed them into my ears. My brain felt muffled. I kept rubbing my neck. My sister began to massage it. "Don't want you to go to sleep!" she screamed. Her voice seemed to come from far away.

"I feel like I'm being hypnotized!"

I thought about raising the snake in kundalini. My spine had garbled the message, and the snake was stuck in my neck. It looked like a huge dried worm.

The rookie Earnhardt blew his engine and came into the pits. Cale Yarborough was still trying to regain the lap he'd lost.

In skydiving, there's a term "whuffo." Whuffos are people who hang around skydivers saying, "Whuffo you want to jump out of a perfectly good airplane?" Now I thought, Whuffo these people want to watch this noise? This isn't fun. It's nuts.

When I was a kid I had a gyroscope toy. It was a wheel mounted inside a ring. If you spun the wheel fast, you could set the ring at odd angles and it would stay balanced. I felt out of balance here on the fourth turn. My psyche was leaning. I watched the tiny cars running inside the thunder. I began to see little black dots swimming around.

Maybe I'm sore from jumping yesterday, I thought. On my second jump my muscles had been cramping from so much adrenaline. Not big muscles, but mean tiny ones in my shoulders, in the undersides of my upper arms.

Two hundred laps. My eyes were too far apart; they wouldn't focus right. I was so tired. The noise hammered at me. It seemed to be inside my head now. Cosmic dentistry.

The roar was in my chest and ass too, and my legs, but at my neck it was still knotted, blocked.

Cale passed Petty. Both were behind Waltrip. Waltrip's car seemed to be faster. Petty passed Cale again. "He's playing with Cale," Roger said.

Waltrip pitted. The crowd screamed. Petty was leading.

I started to shiver. It wasn't cold. I held my legal pad against my chest.

Two hundred sixty laps. I couldn't stand the headache. I decided to take a walk. Warm up. Look for some coffee. Maybe some aspirin.

I had noticed people standing briefly at the railing below, right above the track. I asked Roger about it. "It's all right to do it," he said, "if you can stand it."

I went down the steps and out the aisle, behind the stands. The ground had begun to disappear under litter. There were lines for Cokes and cigarettes. Beer can't be sold on Sunday in South Carolina. The relative silence was startling. Among the drunk men wandering behind the stands there was a randiness, a bald fuck energy that made me nervous.

I walked past the museum, where earlier I'd paid a quarter for a two-minute simulated ride in Richard Petty's car, and bought a sweatshirt that said "Darlington International Speedway." At the main entrance to the speedway was a tiny diner. I got two BC headache powders and a Coke. I sprinkled the powders on my tongue. They tasted like chewed-up aspirin and reminded me of once when I'd opened a cap of psilocybin and sprinkled the powder on a dish of potato salad.

On my way back to my seat I saw some girls handing out little yellow buttons that said "Happy Easter" to the men lined up to use the bathroom. Then the girls asked each man who took a button for a dollar.

The powders took effect quickly. My head felt cottony, pleasant. I was ready.

I went back into the stands, but I didn't go back to my seat. I walked up to the railing. The noise seemed almost visible. I checked the toilet paper in my ears, and then I grabbed the rail with both hands.

The noise ran up my arms, through my shoulders, past my neck, into my head. It ran down my chest, through my waist and hips, down my legs. It came up through my feet. I felt like a tuning fork. I lasted about ten seconds.

When I got back to my seat, I felt wonderful. "Is Petty winning?" I asked.

David Pearson's pit crew had forgotten to fasten his new tires, and when he drove out of pit row they fell off. He rolled into the wall. Petty and Waltrip were still trading the lead. Donnie Allison was gaining on them.

It began to rain. The noise eased while the cars ran under the caution flag. Petty was leading again. "He's going to win under the caution!" Roger said. "They'll call off the race!"

The rain smelled good. I felt good. I didn't want them to call off the race. "Can't they use windshield wipers?"

Roger laughed. "Wipers don't work at 150 miles an hour."

The caution flag was lifted on lap 321. Petty was in the lead. Waltrip passed Petty. "He's got Waltrip where he wants him," Roger said. "He can slingshot around him."

Thirty laps to go. Petty couldn't seem to get around Waltrip. Cale was one lap back but still crowding them. Donnie Allison had almost caught up.

"Petty's testing him," Roger said. "He'll get him. He's setting him up."

On 349, Petty took the lead. Two photographers in the infield began to jump up and down.

I wasn't cold. My head didn't hurt. I couldn't hear myself shouting. I had begun to scream. Everyone was screaming. Everything shook.

On 360, there was a brief caution. The crowd wailed.

With five laps to go, Waltrip and Petty bumper to bumper, they restarted the race. "I'm gonna have an organism!" Roger shouted.

Petty took it on the first turn. Waltrip took it back. Then Petty took it again. On the last lap, Waltrip shot around him and won.

"My man lost!" Roger said. "I almost had a Pontiac arrest!"

The leaders glided by, in the winning order: Darrell Waltrip, Richard Petty, Donnie Allison. Or, as the cars read, Gatorade, STP, and Hawaiian Tanning Butter.

After the Rebel 500, I was drunk and tired. We hung out at the camper for a couple of hours, waiting for the traffic to thin out, and then, although we'd already eaten too much, we stopped at Shoney's on the way back to Charleston. Shoney's is a Southern restaurant chain whose trademark is a huge statue of a huge fat boy wearing huge plaid overalls. Over his head he holds a huge hamburger, like a trophy. The chain's slogan is "Shoney's: Home of the Big Boy."

We had gotten away from the Darlington traffic arteries, and the crowd at Shoney's were on their way home from Sunday-evening church. They held their forks furtively over slices of strawberry pie. "Look how guilty they act," my sister whispered. "They're even afraid to eat."

"This is one group I haven't explored yet," I whispered back. "I hope I can skip them."

I have come home to South Carolina to try to claim my background. I hope I can reclaim what is positive without starting to sing "Rock of Ages" or adopting racist attitudes. The prejudices of white Southerners still startle me.

Recently I went to a wig store in a big shopping mall to

buy a wig for a costume party. "I want a blond afro," I told the matronly lady behind the counter. She was wearing a polyester print dress. She had on stockings and white gloves. She might have been part of the Shoney's church crowd, or a kindergarten teacher.

"They can't make blond afros," she said.

I thought she was kidding. "No, like those black ones over there," I said. "Only I want a blond one."

She looked at me compassionately, even kindly. "You don't understand. They can't make blond afros."

"Wait a minute," I said. "Look at those black afros. They're synthetic, right? And those blond wigs, they're synthetic, right? I want a blond one like that."

There was pity in her eyes. "It's scientific," she said. "They can't make blond afros."

I call this anecdote "the limits of reason." Whether I am with aristocrats, rednecks, or the few blacks I've managed to form tentative friendships with, I am aware that we Southerners do not lead with our intellects. Living here in South Carolina, I am afraid that the critical faculties I worked so hard to develop while I was in New York will turn blue and fall off.

When I stopped trying to pass as a hip suburban housewife, I moved briefly to a commune in Vermont. Then I moved to New York.

In New York I stayed for a month with my friend Penny. Penny was a writer. She had just joined Arica, an organization not entirely dissimilar to Esalen. Penny and I tripped together sometimes. Sometimes we did Arica exercises. Penny rang little brass bells and we sat knees to knees and stared into each other's left eyes. It made us cry.

We both were reading Castaneda. We talked a lot about

paths of knowledge, paths of enlightenment. We drank a lot of wine and smoked dope. "Do you think writing can be a path?" we asked each other. "Do you think a guru is necessary?"

Penny moved to California to work in the Arica organization, and I lost track of her for several years. Then I heard she had left Arica and become a follower of the Indian guru Janaka.

In the mid-seventies, I began to see posters for Janaka around New York. He had opened a temporary ashram on the Upper West Side. I saw an old friend on the street who told me Penny was back in town. She'd left a Janaka poster on his door, beckoning him to an audience with her guru.

I called the ashram and asked for Penny. Penny's doing very important work right now, I was told, but audiences with Janaka are held at such and such a time. I'm not interested in Janaka, I said. I'm interested in my old friend Penny. The woman's voice tinkled gaily in my ear. There's nothing left of Penny that's not Janaka, she said. Penny's been reamed out. I'm coming right over, I said. I want to view the carcass for myself.

The ashram was a brownstone. Penny met me in the hall, and we sat on the steps and talked. "I feel as if I'm living the life you left behind," I said. "I'm writing. I have a good shrink. I give dinner parties."

"Do you think that's a path?" She seemed tired. She smelled of decay. She frightened me.

"It's what I need. I've got this heavy Southern past to drag around." I didn't mention the weight of Penny's past, or of anyone else's past, for that matter. "Do you think this is a path?" I asked. "It reminds me of the Baptist church."

"Oh, I know," she said, and laughed absently.

Penny didn't know that I returned to the ashram the next night. Janaka was giving a group audience. Men and women sat shoeless on different sides of the room. Penny had on a sari. She had a red dot painted on her forehead. There was a purple velvet curtain behind the guru, and some white flowers were on a table in front of it.

I sat in the back and watched Penny chant and pray. I listened to Janaka tell a tale about a man whose guru had sent him to graveyards to curse the dead. How did the dead respond? the guru asked. They did not, master. When you respond as the dead did, Janaka said, you will attain enlightenment.

Penny moved to India, and I have come back to South Carolina to seek a funkier transcendence. Call it the redneck way of knowledge. In my refrigerator is a Mason jar of corn liquor, white lightning. It has raisins in it, which make it taste like a fine rum. When I got home from the Rebel 500 it was past midnight. I was still valiantly drinking Natural Light, but I took out the white lightning to go with it.

I went outside and sat on my front steps. I could hear the ocean moving against the sand a block away. I took a sip of the white lightning. My nervous system was jaded, but the 160-proof liquor was still a rush. It burned cleanly, and warmed me.

I wanted to do something to finish the Rebel 500, but I felt too wiped out. I would have sung "Dixie," but it is a racist song, and anyway I can't sing. I hollered once and threw my beer can across the front yard.

I haven't come back to South Carolina to get religion, but I have come back to a total immersion. If I wash in the blood of the past, I tell myself, maybe I'll be free of it. And something has eased in me, being here these past few months. A pain so constant I thought it was a condition of life has begun to wash away. I feel a sense of peace, of aftermath. "Charleston is where the Ashley and the Cooper rivers meet to form the Atlantic Ocean." I heard that when I was a kid.

I still don't know what it means to love a place, but I know I love the salty mouths of these rivers, I love the smells of the long, mournful marshes, I love these romantic palmettos swaying in this postcard moonlight.

One morning soon after I moved home I got up before sunrise and walked over to the beach. Porpoises rolled in the placid water. Everything was bluish—the sand, the water, the sky. Then the sun came up like an opening, a brilliant tear in the horizon, and for a second I thought I could glimpse through it to another place. I was chanting: *rising, rising, rising.*

Be Here Then

I know how to exaggerate things!" Dixie yelled. "I know how to make a good story!"

I was jammed against my bucket seat. Dixie had the windows and the sunroof open on her Porsche, and we were doing at least ninety on one of the serene highways that run through the Sea Islands below Charleston. We were on our way to the Seabrook Jazz Picnic, an outdoor event that marked the midpoint of Spoleto 1979's sixteen dense days of culture. My hair was whipping my eyes. Oaks arched over us, moss reached down. Azaleas and magnolias blurred by. It was noon, and I'd had two glasses of white wine and a joint for breakfast.

"Drive faster!" I yelled. "I'm gonna stand up!" I scrambled to my feet and raised my head and shoulders through the sunroof. My dark glasses were goggles. The air got hard with speed. I could feel my cheeks rippling back, giving me the vaguely Oriental look skydivers get during freefall. I raised my arms above my head. "I like playing rich kid!" I shouted, but either Dixie didn't hear me or she didn't choose to.

Earlier, Dixie told me a local joke: Charlestonians are like Orientals. They eat rice, worship their ancestors, and speak in a foreign tongue. My face started to feel battered, so I sat back down.

Dixie slowed a bit and lit another joint. "Really, I mean it. I know which things to tell to make a story. You understand what I'm saying?"

"What about the truth?"

"Stories are the truth!"

Dixie is a nineteen-year-old Charleston aristocrat, one of four heirs to an old fortune and an even older name. She is charming, beautiful in an androgynous way, and wild. A long scar runs like a crack down one side of Dixie's face because, when she was twelve, a cousin swiped at her with his great-great-grandfather's Civil War sword. A plastic surgeon tried once to remove this scar, but Dixie won't let anyone try again. "I think it looks dramatic," she says. "I think it shows my, um, heritage." Dixie and her friend Shreve like to bring me stories about their families and other members of the Charleston aristocracy. The rich, they try to show me, decay richly.

"Did Shreve tell you about her brother shooting the television?"

I shook my head, and Dixie nodded happily as she began her tale: "Well, Shreve's little brother was staying at their hunting lodge. Get Shreve to show you the hunting lodge sometime. On the walls of the lodge there are dozens of deer heads, maybe sixty. Shreve doesn't even know who shot them. Her grandfather, probably. Maybe her great-grandfather. But the heads are real old, all of them. And they have aged badly. Some of them have their eyes popping out, and one of them has his lips falling off, and they all look real . . . *personal* about it. Anyway, Shreve's brother was staying there by himself, and he was real lonely. He'd been watching television, but finally he was just too lonely, so he decided to ride into town for some company. On the way to the highway, he hit a fawn with his car. It was knocked out, but it wasn't dead or anything. So he picks this fawn up and brings it back to the lodge. He feels less lonely with this half-conscious baby deer around. He wraps it up for warmth and puts some food beside it and then he goes back to watching TV. Well, you can imagine what happened. This poor little deer wakes up and looks around and sees all her ancestors with their heads mounted on the walls and their eyes popping out and their lips hanging loose, and she freaks. She jumps right through the plate-glass window in the living room. Shreve's brother was so mad he got his shotgun and blew the television away. Bang. Blew it away. This really happened. The TV's out there in the woods, near the lodge. They still use it as a landmark for guests who come to hunt. They tell hunters, Walk down the path through the bamboo stand and turn right at the television."

Southerners are known as storytellers; creative lying is a source of pride. In this account of Spoleto I have taken extreme liberties with the truth, made up incidents and even whole characters, and generally been irresponsible whenever it suited my inscrutable purposes. Spoleto, of course, really happened. Some of this story is true.

HORSES SWEAT, MEN PERSPIRE, WOMEN GLISTEN

Shreve's mother taught her that. It's hot in Charleston, even in late May. The third Spoleto Festival held in the United States began on May 25 and ran through June 10. At a press conference just before the official opening, Gian Carlo Menotti wiped the perspiration from his forehead and complained about press coverage the last two years: "This is a *festival, a celebration* of the arts." Spoleto, he asserted, was not a place for killer critics.

"He couldn't be talking about me," I whispered to Shreve. I had passed Dixie and Shreve off as my official photographers, and Shreve was draped in expensive cameras, as if to prove her legitimacy. "I'm from Charleston. I'm the perfect person to cover Spoleto." I kept feeling like an impostor.

Spoleto is an exercise in the artier arts. Opera, ballet, and classical music dominate, while jazz and more current explorations of dance submit. Actually, the offerings in jazz and modern dance are fairly substantial, and this year's festival also featured an Arthur Miller play. But Spoleto still feels much like an exercise in ancestor worship.

Charleston, being much like an American museum, provides excellent staging. Charleston is not "restored" in the manner of Williamsburg, and it is not "renovated" like San Francisco's Victorian houses. Charleston is preserved, like figs. Take one aristocracy who escaped having their beloved neighborhoods burned by Sherman, stir in the pride of being the folks who fired the first shots of the Civil War, spread this mixture where the mouths of two rivers meet in the lush land of the Lowcountry, and you get Charleston, a city obsessed with itself. Charleston is the only place I've ever been where people talk continually about where they are. The aristocracy sets this tone. Shreve, who is articulate in her fascination and distaste for her own class, says, "They talk about their houses as if the houses were alive. There are actually people in Charleston who don't know that the rest of the world doesn't go hunting on Saturday."

Dixie and Shreve might belong to the St. Cecilia Society, if they weren't women. Women can't belong independently to St. Cecilia, and divorced people can't belong either. St. Cecilia, Charleston's most prestigious organization, has a long waiting list; new members are invited only when a vacancy by death occurs. St. Cecilia's main function is a yearly ball held the second Thursday of January. Dixie was married for a few weeks on an extended drug trip when she was seventeen, so she has never accompanied her family to this grave affair. Shreve's attended several times.

On the way to the opening press conference, she'd been telling me about it. "Guests have to have their names put forward way ahead of time, so they can be checked out socially. Young women can't have escorts who live within one hundred miles of Charleston, because, presumably, if they were the right kind of people for St. Cecilia, they would already belong. And you have to get your dance card filled out ahead of time too. Your dance card, can you believe it? It's waltzes, fox trots, shit like that. We learn these dances in dancing school. They have one cotillion, where everybody dances in lines so they can see who else is there. You have to wear long white gloves, and the debutantes have to wear white. It's all tails and long gowns. They have these marshals running around with special ribbons on who make everybody follow the rules. You can't drink sherry on the punch side of the room—I was reprimanded for that. Women can't go to the bathroom by themselves. Their escorts have to walk them to the bathroom door and wait for them. That's a rule, too."

I grew up a medium-rich kid, but not an aristocrat. One of my grandfathers was a bootlegger. My father was "self-made," and he taught me disrespect for aristocracies, whether of blood or of form. I went to a public high school out on one of the Sea Islands, where most of the students majored in home economics or agriculture, and I wouldn't have been caught dead listening to long-haired music. I thought ballet looked like stilted hopping around and chamber music I associated with chamber pots or torture chambers. Opera was hilarious. I did listen to jazz, but in secret. Now that I'm older and possibly more educated, I've learned that respect for one's elders is not necessarily the same as ancestor worship. Classical forms are not intrinsically pretentious, although the people interested in them may or may not be.

I looked at Spoleto as an opportunity to practice making these distinctions. I also looked at it as a chance to learn more about forms I'm still too ignorant of. However, I kept feeling like an impostor, and as the press conference continued, I realized why. Spoleto is geared for, and largely supported by, rich provincials. I may have grown up a rich kid, but I'm too old for that designation now, and so broke I cried when I found out I'd have to buy new eyeglasses. Suddenly I was armed with $500 in press tickets and a clump of invitations to fancy parties. I was mired in many of the issues I meant to study, and I felt merged with my subject.

When the press conference was over, Shreve and I drove to the College of Charleston for the opening ceremonies. I tried to explain my feelings. "Sure," she said. "Reverse slumming."

Shreve parked her 1960 English Jaguar limousine in a loading zone. She parks wherever she wants to in Charleston, because police seem to be afraid to ticket the black-and-silver Jag. Shreve is tall, angular, has a waist-length braid, and, although she usually wears jeans, looks as if she would own such a car.

"I meant to tell you," she said, as we walked through the College of Charleston's grounds. "The whole point about St. Cecilia is that she was the patron saint of music. St. Cecilia was originally a music society. Doesn't that make Charleston and Spoleto dovetail nicely?"

"I have one for you," I said. "Until the late sixties, students at the C. of C. were required to attend chapel, and in chapel they had to pray, and when they prayed they had to turn around and face south, so none of their prayers would go to the wicked North."

"I already knew that," Shreve said.

We spotted Dixie by the edge of the old cistern, intently photographing the crowd. Hundreds of folding chairs had been placed on the grass, and despite the windless heat, they were being patiently occupied. "These are old-fashioned Charlestonians, aren't they, Shreve. These are downtown natives." I was excited to perceive this quality so clearly. There was a genteel, polite feel to the crowd, a stillness, despite the boredom of waiting for boring speeches. There was more I couldn't name.

"They're the real thing," Shreve said, sounding miserable. "You can tell by all the glistening."

ZEN AND THE
ART OF PARTYING

Spoleto really began later that afternoon, with a party at the Gibbes Art Gallery. My engraved invitation informed me that Mayor Riley was giving this party for Governor Riley. Dressed in our best summer whites, Dixie and I sneaked in a side door to avoid the receiving line. There were several bars scattered through a crowd. "Pace yourself," Dixie warned me as we got our first bourbons. "We've got two more parties and an opera to get through tonight."

I went over to stand by the sandwiches. Dixie began to click pictures. The crowd was a mixture of aristocrats, politicos, press, and young folks who'd cadged invitations so they could make the scene. My press badge made it legitimate for me not to talk to anyone. The only person I knew was Dixie, although I did see the woman who cuts my hair.

A man and a woman came in wearing Bermuda shorts, dark glasses, rubber flip-flops, and press passes. I went over and introduced myself. Rosemary and Ed were from a national wire service. They were already drunk. "This is dreadful," Rosemary said. "Let's go on to the press party at the Edmondston-Alston house."

Soon the four of us were piled intimately into Dixie's Porsche, smoking what Ed called a Texas joint since it was as thick as a thumb. "I love illegal substances," Rosemary said, and I wondered how I'd ended up with this woman in my lap. As the dope loosened my muscles and spread an almost involuntary sense of well-being, I wondered even more.

The Edmondston-Alston house is on East Battery, the most prestigious location in Charleston's most prestigious neighborhood. Three piazzas run the length of the house and provide an unobstructed view of Charleston Harbor. The house, which was built in the 1820s and 1830s, is maintained as a museum and open daily to tourists, who pay $1.75 each to listen to riffs about the woodwork and the furniture and the silver and the view.

The bartender poured me a full glass of Jack Daniel's, and between that and the Texas joint, I had begun to feel just fine. I went upstairs to the second-floor piazza and leaned against the railing. The harbor, like the house, seemed peaceful, graceful, and permanent. From houses like this one, early Charlestonians watched the shelling that began the Civil War as if it were a momentous fireworks display.

Soon Rosemary joined me. "How old is your friend Dixie?" she asked while we watched sailboats.

"Nineteen. Are you from Charleston?"

"Michigan. Isn't she a little young for you?"

I looked at this Rosemary. "Dixie's my friend. You think I'm a chicken hawk, huh?"

Rosemary shrugged. "They told me all Southerners like chicken."

We were both leaning on the piazza railing very consciously now. My tumbler of bourbon had mostly disappeared. Rosemary looked uncertain. "If a piece of fried chicken falls in the forest and no one hears it," she said, "does it make a sound?"

"Not bad," I conceded. "Not bad at all."

Dixie appeared on the street below. "Hey, girl!" she called to me. "Let's go do this opera!"

The Desperate Husband, by Domenico Cimarosa, was performed at Gaillard Municipal Auditorium. Gaillard is a modern salmon-colored building with smoked-glass windows. Someday Gaillard Auditorium will be a period piece like the Edmondston-Alston house, just as someday pink plaster flamingos will be in museums.

The Desperate Husband would have been the first opera I'd ever seen. However, the first act seemed particularly bizarre after the two parties I'd been to; I slept through the second act.

Dixie took me out to the car, where we inhaled another joint and some more-expensive substances. Dixie calls this powdering her nose.

I felt wonderful by the time we reached the party at the Customs House. I don't remember much of it except for some impressively molded shrimp pastes and the lovely geometric tiles on the floor. Dixie said I told entertaining stories to a number of people, but I think she was being polite, because later, when she dropped me off at my house, she said, "Girl, you been in the North too long. You better learn how to party, or you'll never make it through sixteen days of this."

PERIOD PIECES

"Irony is the ability to look at yourself clearly and still get the joke." Shreve punctuated this remark by pouring her glass of wine slowly across her tennis shoe.

We were sitting on the steps of the Dock Street Theatre. In a few minutes we would see the opening of *The Medium*, a two-act opera written and directed by Spoleto's founder, Gian Carlo Menotti. Well-dressed people stared at us, but Shreve seemed singularly unself-conscious in her tennis shoes, jeans, and silk shirt. Her Jaguar limousine slouched nonchalantly at the curb.

"Did you make that expression up?" I asked.

"Yep. That's what happens when you send a plantation girl to Vassar. They get witty on you." But Shreve seemed unhappy. She'd been looking restless, dissatisfied for the last few weeks.

When I first returned to Charleston, Shreve and Dixie were among the first people I met. "We're the Dixiecrats!" Shreve sang at me, hanging on to Dixie to stay vertical. "We believe in the one-party system! We just party all the time!"

I met them at the Garden and Gun Club, a Spoleto-spawned disco that has become the year-round hip place in town. The Garden and Gun Club occupies what was once the J. C. Penney's, where I bought my first bra. It was near closing time, and we were all in that favored altered state of Southerners, inebriation.

I was fascinated by Dixie and Shreve, who had the unmistakable aura of Charleston bluebloods. Their brittleness and wit about class were indicators, as was their easy self-assurance. So were expensively casual clothes, orthodontist-designed teeth, and sports cars. This was before I'd seen

Shreve's limousine (she used to drive a hearse), before I'd seen Dixie's family house in the neighborhood south of Broad Street (this area is called S.O.B. by less wellborn natives), and before I'd seen Shreve's plantation on the Ashley River.

The first thing I noticed about Dixie was her white scar. Then I noticed the no-makeup beauty, and the nearly faultless sense of style. "Style is just confidence," Dixie once told me, trying to explain how she can wear a man's sleeveless undershirt with pleated linen pants, and look as if she's getting ready to be photographed for a fashion magazine.

Shreve's long face cannot match Dixie's beauty, but Shreve's eyes have a quality of looking inward. Even high, Shreve looks thoughtful. Once she climbed through my apartment window at six in the morning screaming, "LET'S GO SWIMMING! GET UP, GIRL!" When I staggered into the living room without my glasses, we were both stopped by an abrupt, intense eye contact. "Sorry," she said, and I made her a cup of coffee before she left. After that I always felt closer to Shreve.

The problems of inheritance are not the exclusive province of the rich or highborn. Many of us who thought of ourselves as radicals in the sixties have begun to inherit the things we revolted against. Jerry Rubin is a huckster, Abbie Hoffman bores just about everybody, and Rennie Davis, I heard, sells insurance. (If that rumor's not true, it ought to be.) Bob Dylan's gums are receding. Joan Baez has criticized the North Vietnamese. In a confused moment, I recently bought a cemetery plot. We inherit more than money and blood. We inherit the past; we inherit expectations; we may even inherit attitudes. Inheritance is a tricky business, as the number of ex-Catholics among s & m freaks indicates.

While we sat on the steps of the Dock Street Theatre, Shreve looked very far away. I asked her a question I ask a lot of people lately. Why does she think storytelling is so important to Southerners?

"Well, my dear, I'm still trying to figure that one out."

"Come on, Shreve."

Shreve always sounds uncomfortable without the defense of sarcasm. "I don't know, the Civil War, maybe. The winners write history and the losers write poetry and all that. But that view's not original with me. Anyway, I think storytelling was important in the South before the Civil War. Spellbinding, maybe. Wishful thinking. The love of illusion. This is one hell of a romantic place. What do you think?"

I would have liked to tell her what stories mean in my family. My mother and sister and I tell each other the same stories over and over. This repetition is an incantation, an invocation of the beauties of patina, and a way of expressing complicated feelings about each other. With our tales we entertain, comfort, make order, instruct, chastise, and preserve.

Stories stretch. They exaggerate, make larger than life, freeze moments, name them, move them outside the present. Storytelling is one opposite of *Be Here Now*, but storytelling is not abstract. Storytelling is *Be Here Then*. This is why, in fiction, the past tense reads as if it were the present, while the present tense creates a dreamlike feeling.

A buzzer signaled performance time. Shreve and I went inside and took our seats. The Dock Street Theatre is a creepy, lovely reconstruction of an early Georgian playhouse. "I'm excited to see this," Shreve said. "Dixie saw it in rehearsal and it scared Jesus right out of her." But, as the lights dimmed, I looked hard at Shreve's face again. Maybe life under the one-party system isn't all that pleasant.

THE MEDIUM IS THE QUESTION

The Medium is a two-act chamber opera about a fraudulent medium. Madame Flora supports herself, her daughter Monica, and Toby, a mute orphan boy she has befriended, by staging séances for guileless people. In one of these séances Madame Flora is touched on the back of the neck by someone. Or she thinks she is.

Madame Flora goes mad trying to understand this moment. Did she really raise the dead? When she exposes her false operation to her patrons, they insist they have been experiencing actual communications. "You thought you were cheating, but you were not. You were not." Madame Flora then begins to suspect Toby of having tricked her; it was Toby who had sneaked into the dark and put his hand on her.

Whether the dead can speak is unresolved in *The Medium*, but we have no similar doubt about Toby's muteness. When Madame Flora, holding a pistol, sings to Toby, "If you are human, answer me," he cannot reply. Madame Flora kills him in a frenzy of release, and doesn't recognize him as she gloats over his body.

I went to see *The Medium* twice. I still can't understand why an artist would try to marry music with storytelling, and I don't know enough about opera to judge singing, but *The Medium* was staged wonderfully, and Beverly Evans, as Madame Flora, was hypnotic, charismatic, anguished, and terrifying. The illusion-within-illusion, like the story-within-a-story, is an old trick but still an effective one. Madame Flora's fake séances strengthen our belief in her reality; when the fakery of the séances is called into question, we are drawn further into the illusion. And having a mute in an opera is an interesting idea.

Whether the dead can speak is a question one can ask about opera as well as human beings. Opera, like fox hunting, is more of a cult than a living form. There may have been artistic justification for singing *The Desperate Husband*, but there wasn't a similar justification for staging it. *The Medium* is a good play. As good a play, in fact, as Arthur Miller's *The Price*, which I saw the next night.

The next day I went to the Ballet Repertory Company and a chamber music concert. I also went to two parties. Then I went to see the Douglas Norwick Dancers and the Bill Evans Dance Company and two more chamber music recitals. And two more parties. I stopped eating anything other than breakfast and hors d'oeuvres. I interviewed Beverly Evans, who remarked that Charleston smelled like a cemetery. I interviewed Douglas Norwick, whose dance troupe I admired. If the Norwick dancers were quirky and entertaining, the Bill Evans Dance Company provided a leaden comparison. I will remember them best for "Impressions of Willow Bay," in which the company waved their arms around a lot.

The chamber music series made my mornings magical and educational. There were a lot of these concerts, and I went to as many as I could. I discovered that I love the intimacy and seriousness of chamber music, and I appreciated the Spoleto mixture of classical works with those of more modern composers. I did have one bad moment in the chamber music series, when an experimental piece was being performed. While the oboist was earnestly playing Luciano Berio's *Sequenza*, I was trying just as earnestly to understand the piece. Then I realized it reminded me of a large fly whining around a silent room. I began to laugh helplessly. I saw a man two rows in front of me turn purple and bury his face in his program while tears of hilarity ran down his cheeks.

Spoleto became a blur. I remember a mint julep party on South Battery. Mint juleps are made of sugar syrup, bruised

mint, and bourbon. Crushed ice, no water. I remember waiting to use the bathroom in the Dock Street Theatre and
watching, through the space at the bottom of the stall door,
a woman roll down her rubber girdle. The heat wore away
at everything. Strings popped on instruments. Dampers jammed. At the Seabrook Jazz Picnic I watched a man drip onto
the fried chicken he was eating. When the Alvin Ailey
dancers came to perform three different programs, I only
made it to two. The last piece I recall seeing involved three
women dancing the parts of a pinball machine. It was called
"Tilt."

GONE WITH THE TIDE

I gave away my last Ailey tickets and went to Folly Beach to
think about alligators. When I was a kid in Charleston, we
didn't have problems with alligators. It's true that my sister
and I once found a skull out in the ruined rice paddies behind our house, but I never saw a living 'gator.

In the sixties alligators were put on the endangered species
list, and they've made a comeback. Shreve has seen them in
the lakes landscaped into her grounds. Corpses of 'gators
who've been hit by cars can be found on Highway 17. My
brother, who lives in the country, had one of his dogs eaten.
A woman named Becky Lee wrote to the *News and Courier*
when her fourteen-year-old daughter, swimming off their
private dock, was chased and nearly caught by a ten-foot
'gator. When, Becky Lee asked, does an endangered species
become a dangerous species? I think this is a legitimate question to ask about aristocracies as well as alligators.

I'm not against national parks, and I'm not against aristocracies, as long as they're reasonably contained. I think we should preserve our classical resources. Spoleto is a national park of the arts, where old forms waddle around exhibiting new life. Spoleto is not only a celebration of the arts, it is a commemoration of them, which is why a nasty debate about the artistic legitimacy of jazz could even happen.

I went to Folly Beach to think about these things because Folly Beach is washing away. The front beach at Folly was once the site of opulent summer residences. Now the first two streets are gone, except for two old houses which stand on stilts out in the water. When I was growing up, we used to climb into the abandoned houses to drink and smoke dope. Now walkways have been built out to them, and one has become a bar and restaurant called Atlantic House.

There are many programs to save Folly Beach. Stone breakwaters have been built into the water every hundred yards or so, to try to prevent the sand from washing away. In even rather ordinary storms waves break against retaining walls, and against houses. Most of the pier washed away in the hurricane that hit Charleston in the late fifties. Another hurricane might tear off a few more blocks of Folly Beach and destroy it once and for all.

When I got to the beach it was low tide. The waves had receded far from the spindly stilts of Atlantic House, and the breakwaters were exposed like sharp stone teeth along the gummy ridge of the ocean's mouth.

I bought a beer and sat on the railing of the veranda. At the end of *Gone With the Wind* Scarlett O'Hara hears her father's voice intoning, "Nothing lasts but the land." In this dead sea-level town, built on what was once the ocean's bottom, even the land feels doubtful. As I looked up and down the naked beach, I thought I could see, like transparencies, the vanished houses.

I called Shreve and told her to crawl through my apartment window and take the rest of the press tickets. I didn't have the heart for any more Spoleto.

I stayed out at Folly the rest of the evening, getting down. I drank, thought, and listened to classical Southern beach music: Sam Cooke, the Drifters, Fats Domino, Tommy Edwards, the Platters, the Coasters, and Mary Wells.

ALLIGATOR STAMPEDE
A HOAX

Or so the Charleston papers said, retracting their story of the day before. I don't know if Rosemary caused this confusion with something she sent out over her wire service, or whether the local papers fouled up on their own. Dixie and I were just pulling Rosemary's leg, and at the time she seemed to understand that. At any rate, I am the only person who knows what really happened concerning the alligators at the Seabrook Jazz Picnic, because I caused the trouble.

The newspapers said there were a dozen alligators at the Seabrook Jazz Picnic, but there was only one. And there wasn't any stampede, animal or human, just a rather rapid disassembling of the audience, partly because of the rain.

The Seabrook Jazz Picnic was held on a golf course at Seabrook Island. To shade the performers, a platform reminiscent of the ones at graveside funerals had been set up on the trimmed grass. Dixie and I arrived at the Jazz Picnic, grabbed our cooler, and went to find Shreve.

The crowd was laid out very orderly. At one edge of the fairway fried chicken, hot dogs, and hamburgers were for sale. At the other edge was a water hazard with a tiny sign that said, "Beware of the Alligators."

We found Shreve with some friends who were already staggering around. Dixie and I opened a bottle of Pescadou, a wine we tell each other makes people crazy. Since the Jazz Picnic was the midpoint of Spoleto, we were not yet showing the strain of overindulgence.

It was a hot, overcast day. The air was humid and thick and there was no breeze at all. Soon we were all drenched with glistening. The crowd listened patiently to Za Zu Zaz, but acoustically a golf course leaves a lot to be desired. Dixie sat on the ground and began to do strenuous yoga-based exercise. Her energy was so high she looked like someone loosening up to go berserk.

Shreve and I were talking, and Dixie got bored. "I can make anybody believe anything," she bragged.

"Think storytelling is a dead form?" I asked Shreve.

Shreve was sprawled on the ground now too. "Nope. Aristocrats are a dead form."

"Storytelling," Dixie said, "will live as long as I do."

That's when we saw Rosemary coming toward us. "Isn't that the woman who called me a piece of chicken?" Dixie asked.

"It's a good thing you've got on that shirt," she said, pointing at the Lacoste alligator on Rosemary's blue V-neck.

"Why?"

Dixie gestured toward the sign by the water hazard. "Didn't you see the alligators in that pond? They stock it. They bring up these special tame alligators from Hilton Head. Makes the golf course more colorful."

Rosemary looked at me and I nodded.

"They thought maybe they should round them up before the Jazz Picnic," Dixie continued. "There was a big argument about it. They had a golfer lose some digits."

"Digits?" Rosemary said.

Dixie nodded and held up her hand. "Two digits. Looking for his golf ball over there in the reeds. Lost his nine iron too." When Rosemary let the nine-iron remark go by, Dixie said, "And I guess you know what happened with the alligators at the Easter sunrise services. The ones at Charles Towne Landing. That was a real stampede. The alligators attacked everyone except those in Lacoste shirts. I don't know why."

Rosemary smiled. "I see I'm being took."

"Don't you like it?" I asked.

"Ah reckon," Rosemary said.

Shreve and I left Rosemary talking to Dixie. We sat down and listened to the music for an hour or so. Between the heat and the alcohol, I was beginning to feel as if my mind was dripping out of my ears.

I decided to go find a bathroom. There were portable johns by the water hazard. In my muddled state, it seemed terribly important to find out whether there really were alligators in that pond. I thought the warning sign was for dramatic purposes only.

With the deliberate steps of the thoroughly drunk, I walked up and down the water's edge, searching through the reeds. "I'm looking for this alligator," I told two serene couples who had spread a picnic blanket under a tree.

Then I saw him. Or her. Or it. Maybe I'd been looking straight at him for a while. He was right there in the marsh grass. Only his eyes were showing, and a portion of his back. I kept staring at him, half hidden there. He didn't move and I didn't either. I stared at him a long time, and he seemed to be staring back. Well, I thought, maybe he just wants some attention. His eyes seemed cunning and vulnerable, if knobby.

A man was standing beside me. He was wearing tennis shorts and a lemon-colored golf visor. He had a beard. "I don't think this is a good idea," he said quietly.

"What are you," I asked, "a psychiatrist or something?"

But he made me feel ridiculous, so I turned away. I guess the alligator felt as close to me as I did to him, because when

I turned to go, he followed me out of the reeds onto the fairway.

The crowd rippled, tensed near its edge. Too much was made of this incident. It wasn't a big alligator. It was just that people began to panic because the alligator was squatting there, gazing at the crowd with those headlamp eyes. "Get that alligator out of here!" a red-faced man yelled at me. Then somebody threw a volleyball at the 'gator. It bounced off his back and he retreated swiftly into the water.

Rumors were racing through the crowd. Abruptly it began to rain. The audience and the performers left fast. I started to laugh and couldn't stop.

In the downpour I poked through the debris the picnickers had left. I easily found what I was looking for. It was an abandoned Lacoste shirt, the classic white kind.

"THIS IS DIXIE!" boomed over the sound system. "I HAVE A BAD ATTITUDE! I WAS BORN WITH A BAD ATTITUDE AND I INTEND TO KEEP IT! THIS IS DIXIE!"

I made my way through the rain and trash to the stage. Dixie was pacing up and down the platform with the microphone in one hand and a bottle of Moët in the other. Shreve was sitting, dazed and wet, on the edge.

Dixie handed me the champagne. "Did you know those assholes are saying a dozen alligators came onto the fairway? I made that story up, and now they all think it's true. Where'd you get that shirt?"

I took a slug of the champagne. "Found it," I said. "Totemic protection. From aristocrats."

Dixie took the bottle back and poured some of the champagne on my head. "You're safe now, kiddo. Did you really eyeball an alligator to start this mess? That's what Shreve heard."

I grinned and shrugged. "You know how Southerners exaggerate things."

A Thousand Words
About a Picture

The map on the front page of the Charleston newspaper resembled a game board. Hurricane David was moving across the Caribbean, and curved black arrows showed the storm's path. The Dominican Republic was the probable target; Charleston was not even part of the picture.

I took my morning coffee, a cane pole, and a can of worms down to the dock. I like to catch bream while I'm waking up.

My cousin Matt was raking pine straw out of the volley-ball court next door. Matt is a trial lawyer, and his trained voice could make "Gimme your threes" sound authoritative. "That hurricane is going to hit us!" he boomed richly.

I never argue with Matt. "Okay," I said, and went fishing.

That night David slid his marker across the Dominican Republic. A lot of people drowned. The morning newspaper showed him aiming toward Miami. Miami is six hundred miles from Charleston. The day was brilliantly hot.

Cousin Carl came over with his wife's Ad Lib set. Ad Lib is

a game with little letters on dice. You roll the dice, turn over a sand-glass timer, and make as many words as you can. "Denise said you wanted to check your timer against hers." Carl is a professor at the medical university. "Did you see the papers? That hurricane is coming here."

Patty, my sister, was studying a parlay card. Parlay cards cost five dollars each. You pick ten winners of football games according to point spreads printed on the card. If you hit nine out of ten, you win a hundred dollars. "Yeah," she said without looking up. "We're due."

Two days later, Charleston was part of the picture. David bounced against Florida, then headed straight toward us. The twenty-five members of my family secured the beach houses as best we could and returned to our houses in town.

When I woke up early Tuesday, the rain and wind had arrived. The eye was scheduled for 7 p.m. By midmorning tornadoes were spotted near the Wappoo Bridge. For an hour the air turned yellow.

I taped the windows, then went to the grocery store for staples. Mother baked a ham. Patty got out the oil lamps, flashlights, and candles. My friend Wright arrived, carrying cameras and an electric popcorn popper. "Apocalypse soon," she sang.

"This is real life," I said, but I didn't mean it. My family has always loved games.

When I first left Charleston for college many years ago, logic was my favorite game. Logic seemed comfortably hopeless, like solitaire. I spent my free time quantifying letters-to-the-editor from the local newspapers into the equations of logic. This exercise in irreducible irrationality helped me relax.

In philosophy class they taught me that Immanuel Kant's habits were so precise his neighbors could set their watches by his daily walks. I soon lost interest in philosophy. If Kant was so rigid, he had to be leaving out a great deal. I lived in a world of dreams and hallucinations. Logic was a Band-Aid on my burgeoning mind. Soon I had a nervous breakdown.

Looking back, I understand that I saw the metaphorical connection between Kant's life and his work as more important than the work itself. I still hold this view. What logic can't grasp metaphor can. Metaphor is the hand thrust under the water, catching living fish. Metaphor is a passageway between fantasy and logic; it will take you someplace new.

My sister fingered the baked ham dreamily. "I bet it'll be worse than when Gracie hit. I bet it'll be worse than Camille in New Orleans. Maybe we'll spend the night on the roof."

The wind built. The power went off. The phone died. It rained thickly. We ate sandwiches and drank bourbon. We played gin, Ad Lib, Spite and Malice, and hearts. We listened to a transistor radio. David would hit at high tide. "Charleston might wash away," Mother said, shaking the dice.

Around four o'clock we heard a whirring sound, a rumble above the wind. Through the taped windows we watched a large tree in the backyard pull free of the earth and lie down on its side.

Carefully Mother discarded. "Must have been a little twister."

Wright and I went onto the back porch. The porch was a capsule inside the wind and rain. I kept walking to the violent edge and letting the wind blow me back. I decided not to crawl out to the downed tree.

Wright, protecting her lens with her hand, was taking pictures.

"I can do around the world with a yo-yo." The wind erased my voice. I continued, much louder, "I can do more than one hundred with a fly bat! I can do jacks from one to ten without a mistake! I play good marbles!"

"What are you saying?" Wright shouted. "I can't hear you!"

I leaned over the railing. My face was drenched. I screamed, "I can wiggle my ears!"

David hit Savannah, an hour south, and held there. The wind began to limp. The rain slowed. Charleston was the woman in the circus the knife thrower barely misses.

The power was still off, and probably would be for several days. Patty and Mother were playing duplicate Ad Lib by hurricane lamp. The dark crowded over them.

"It could have been a lot worse," Mother said.

"David was a dud," Patty said.

"It's all in the game," Wright said.

Patty asked Wright why she was taking pictures of the coffee table, and Wright said a picture was worth a thousand words.

John Paul's
Passion Play

I first glimpsed John Paul II on television. He was blessing handicapped children in Ireland. "Do the children pray to God? I'm sure their prayers go straight to heaven." Unexpectedly, I began to cry. I found my reaction unsophisticated, not to mention threatening.

I called my friend Arthur, an ex-Catholic ex-Marxist. I hoped to say something clever, but instead I said, "I'm so confused about God."

Arthur was watching the same newscast. "You and everybody else."

"I thought religion was supposed to be the opiate of the people."

I could feel Arthur shrug. "This is the age of drugs."

It was the end of the seventies. It was the end of the second millennium since the death of Jesus. It was the end of the age of Pisces. No one knew yet what it might be the beginning of. Einstein and Freud were dead. The moon had been demystified with spaceships, heaven penetrated with telescopes, radio signals, and jabbing rockets. Astronomy was fast and strange, sounding more and more like metaphysics. Time as a constant collapsed along with Newton's laws. The only certainty was the speed of light, the only apotheosis the shattering flashes at Hiroshima and Nagasaki.

This was the context for the resurrection of the Pope.

I went early to mass at Yankee Stadium. Through a logistic mixup, I couldn't get into the press box. I took my bottle of wine and dinner from Balducci's to a "Special Lounge," where I arranged to watch the services with a dozen policemen.

The good-looking plainclothesman beside me was from the Bronx arson squad. First, he told me the Pope would be running an hour late, then he told me there was a cop under the altar as well as a fireman and a stretcher. Then he told me he had been an undercover narcotics agent, but he wouldn't have busted people for marijuana, "I just wouldn't, that's all," or for personal amounts of cocaine. Then he told me he was a Catholic, but he didn't go to church anymore. He showed me rosaries in his pocket sent by cousins, aunts, uncles to be made more holy by proximity to the Pope.

The sea of faithful stretched below us. The Special Lounges, which range between the second and third tiers, gave me an insight into assassination as target practice. The unlighted lounges looked out onto the brightly lighted stadium like gun slits in a fort. The red plastic that covered the altar and the tiny chair throne the Pope would occupy looked like figments from a penny arcade.

But this was Yankee Stadium, and the Pope's coat of arms was on the scoreboard.

"This is wonderful, isn't it?" the cop volunteered.

"Yeah," I said and meant it.

"It's like, it's like a world series of the Holy Spirit."

Cab driver who brought me in from La Guardia: *I'm not religious, but my wife's Catholic, she was this cute little girl, she wanted to get married in the Church, I couldn't break her heart, I signed one of those things saying I'd raise one of my kids Catholic, I don't mind. What I do mind, every night she gets in bed and crosses her legs and prays and prays. I say stop, you don't have to pray so much, she says you're an animal, you don't believe in God, I say I do believe in God, especially when I'm in trouble, the rest of the time I can take care of myself.*

I had arrived an hour early, the Pope would be an hour late, so I asked the cops to watch my bag and went back outside the stadium. Crowds still poured swiftly through the gates. I stood on the sidewalk awhile, enjoying the polite, urgent movement, the shining faces, and a sense of goodness that was almost tangible. To those who had been lucky enough to get tickets, Yankee Stadium was church, and this was the biggest Sunday of their lives.

There were others crowded against the barricades who looked, not angry, but broken-hearted. I talked to a cross-eyed, crew-cut man wearing a button with a picture of Jesus on it. "I don't care what they say, when the Pope starts to give Communion, I'm going in there, period. I've got to go in there." I asked if he was willing to fight the police. He shook his head desperately, then closed his eyes. "I've got to go in there," he said again, as if need were a method of teletransportation.

Out of curiosity I spent twenty minutes looking for scalpers and didn't find any. I did find some duplicitous Hare Krishnas panhandling, and I did find two teenage boys with only one ticket between them, who, rather than be separated, sold it to a middle-aged man.

At two of the entrance gates, the band of lights at the top of the stadium appeared as part of a brilliant diadem. When people turned in to the entrances they were often startled. "I think that's in really bad taste," one nervous man said to his wife.

"Wow," I heard two different nuns say.

Then a little boy, maybe six or seven years old, said, "Look, mama!" He pointed at the stadium lights and raised both arms above his head as if he were witnessing a miracle.

Everybody knows how the light of reason lifted us out of ignorance and darkness. Everybody knows how the rise of science debunked superstition.

I am the light, the truth, and the way.

If, in the Western world, Christianity was once a light we held against suffering and death, if once the Bible was human-kind's only encyclopedia, rationality casts revealed religion into the dark it once assuaged. To put this quite a different way, after Darwin, punching holes in the biblical version of history was like shooting fish in a barrel. Biology made the Virgin Birth seem silly. Two things I remember from my childhood in the fifties: the phrase "God is dead" and the ditty "I don't care if it rains or freezes long as I got my plastic Jesus."

My parents did take me to church. First I was a Baptist, then a Methodist, then a Presbyterian, depending on our neighborhood. In adolescence I rebelled against my upcoming baptism by going to the Catholic church for six months or so, guiltily contemplating conversion. If Methodist doctrine seemed like nonsense, in the Catholic church I couldn't even understand what they were saying. But I found the Latin and the ancient music and the religious statues comforting. Catholicism embraced mystery. I could feel the weight of history pressing through it, and I could feel the validation of my own growing conviction that the inner world, those areas of the mind not accessible to reason, were more important than what my eyes could see. What I mean is, the Catholic church set off in me the same resonances, echoes, and prismatic glimpses that my budding sexuality did.

In his book *Take a Bishop Like Me*, Paul Moore, the Episcopal bishop, discusses the possibility that religious emotion and sexual feeling come from the same mysterious depths. Certainly the sexual revolution contributed to the decline of Christianity's popularity. Contraception dissolved the bond between orgasm and reproduction. Sex is natural, the new morality proclaimed, and guilt over it is a drag.

By my late teens religiosity struck me as embarrassingly unenlightened, and Catholicism, I thought, was the dumbest of all. "I don't care if it rains or freezes . . ."

When I got married at the age of eighteen, I had a sense of sex as holy. When I got divorced seven years later, I still thought sex was holy, but that marriage was part of the property system. It was an institution whose very nature ran counter to deep personal meaning. Like, say, organized religion. Or belonging to a sorority.

Later I lived with a woman for several years, and if I no longer thought sex was sacred, I did think it was the most important thing that could happen between me and another person. Sex was the inner world, an altered state; it was speaking in tongues.

In the time I've lived alone, I've taken religion more and more seriously. Religious ecstasy no longer seems like something to sneeze at, and orgasm, well, I'm no longer sure it's more important than a sneeze.

Sex is a biological drive, a hunger, a pleasure, and a need, but I doubt it is a path. That sexuality could involve transcendence seems like something I once dreamed. A naïve, lovely idea, like the divinity of Jesus.

Jesus died at thirty-three, which is a pervasively bad age for the protagonists of novels. Like Bob Dylan, I've managed to outlive Jesus. Unlike Bob Dylan, I'm not sure I have to serve somebody. However, when I returned to South Carolina to live out that thirty-third year, it was with a deliberate sense of seeking rebirth. I wanted to acknowledge the mystery of blood.

My marriage, my friendships, and the commune I once lived in never replaced the special feeling I had with my family. I like hanging out with people made out of the same substance I am. It's nice to see my dead father's ghost in my brother's slouching walk, to see my grandmother's chin in my sister's face, my own teenage hopefulness in a picture of my mother in her youth. My brother, sister, and I are variations on a genetic theme. Through my kin I glimpse the possibility of inherited memory. My wish to believe in God feels blood-induced. In outliving Jesus, I haven't managed to outgrow him.

A Jungian psychologist once told me that religion was like a hole in the psyche. If God is dead, the need for God is not. With the decline of organized religion in this country (the Catholics lost twelve million members in the last dozen years), the quest for supranatural experience has manifested itself in other ways: in a fascination with gurus, in a national obsession with UFOs, in belief in the Bermuda Triangle, in religious claims for psychedelic drugs, in the popularity of astrology, reincarnation, aura reading, the *I Ching*, mediums, hypnosis, and the branches of parapsychology. Recently, an intelligent man tried to explain to me how pyramids could sharpen razors. The shroud of Turin has been scientifically examined to explore the possibility (among others equally bizarre) that Jesus was a spaceman and the shroud was marked through some sort of photographic process when his spaceship called him home.

We've been needing a miracle. Traditionally, Popes have been old, dull, and Italian. Popes said *we* instead of *I* and made pious pompous announcements. The advent of John Paul II, the Polish poet, actor, and scholar, who speaks half a dozen languages, uses the first person singular, and smiles with wonderful warmth, is creating a surge of vitality within the Catholic church. It is as if one of the statues in the cathedral had gotten down off its pedestal and started addressing the crowd. Or the plastic Jesus on the dashboard smiled and said hello. John Paul II has the power to make people feel individually addressed. He is a media master, and he's gotten the kind of exposure Jesus could never have hoped for.

I went to one of the baseball bars next to the stadium. The balding bartender was wearing a John Paul T-shirt stretched across his big belly. "Are you Catholic?" I asked. "Nah," he said. "I just like the Pope, that's all."

The man sitting beside me clutched his ticket. He put his beer down and touched me lightly on the arm. "We're so lucky to be here," he said. I thought I could see, in his eyes, the ways he had been hurt. "This is like history tonight. This is the greatest man since Jesus."

Bag lady in Washington, D.C.: *The nuns told me I didn't have no love in me, they told me I wouldn't ever love nobody, but I fixed them, old dried-up penguins, they look like pen-*

guins, well, I seen God and they haven't. I really seen him, you believe me? I seen him in these flashes of light.

When I got back to the Special Lounge, they were announcing over the P.A. system the plans for distributing the Host. Priests with leftover wafers should bring them to the Yankee dressing room, which was serving as the sacristy.

I seemed to be getting more and more nervous. I opened my chicken pesto and poured a glass of wine. Maybe if I chowed down, I wouldn't be hungry for the Host.

I asked my good-looking friend from the arson squad who made the wafers. He told me he was pretty sure nuns did. I guess even the brides of Christ have to bake the bread.

I kept staring at the altar near second base. Football and baseball have become (in the same decades in which church attendance has declined) partial replacement for religion. Instead of God on Sunday morning, it's the game on Sunday afternoon. Spectator sports are ritualized public releases, and if football is closer to the extreme physicality of holy rollers, baseball is closer to the slow, mysterious repetitions of Catholicism. Baseball is boring to the uninitiated, but to its devotees it's a subtle world of mental excellences, concentration, asceticism, and tradition. Baseball cards aren't so different from saints' cards. All this is by way of saying that for this particular mass I think the setting mattered.

Two women leaned over the first balcony holding up a sign that said "Holy Trinity Dunkers."

The red-jacketed ushers were the same unionized guys who always work the stadium.

Hawkers walked through the hushed crowd yelling, "Soda, Soda!"

"LADIES AND GENTLEMEN! PLEASE TAKE YOUR SEATS! CLEAR THE WARNING TRACK!"

Everyone sat down while some bishops and cardinals marched in.

I noticed a white dog down near the Yankee dugout. The man holding the leash kept petting the dog and whispering to it. Later I found out this dog sniffs explosives. But, when I asked my ex-undercover man, he said, "I don't know. Couldn't be a police dog. You wouldn't want to pet ours."

I thought of the black dogs of hell in *The Omen*, an unintentionally hilarious horror movie about the devil. "Maybe that's the Pope's dog."

"I doubt it," the cop said. "Even if he had one, I don't think he'd bring it."

"God is a concept by which we measure our pain."—"God," by John Lennon. "Jesus died for somebody's sins but not mine."—"Gloria," as sung by Patti Smith. I fortified myself against the coming of the Pope.

"PLEASE CLEAR THE WARNING TRACK!"

The crowd sighed like a single organism. The music built dramatically, solemnly. The crowd rose to its feet, as if sensing the Pope rising through the stadium.

A procession of bishops and cardinals began. They were wearing white robes and white helmets, and from the back they looked like Ku Klux Klansmen. When they reached their seats they took off their hats, which are called miters, and replaced them with skull caps.

Everything was in place except the Pope. Only the angel was missing from the Christmas tree.

"PLEASE CLEAR THE WARNING TRACK!"

"That's the third annunciation," I said. "He'll show up soon."

Triumphal entry music boomed over the P.A. system. The gates behind center field opened; phalanxes of uniformed policemen walked through. The triumphal entry music continued. Next came a large group of Secret Service men wearing dark suits, earphones, and worried expressions.

John Paul II entered and began a slow circling of the stadium as if he were a homecoming queen. The Popemobile is a Bronco jeep, which I suppose is as close as you can get to a donkey in the age of automobiles.

The Pope waved and blessed the crowd. People with tickets for the infield ran beside the car. Everyone cheered and applauded with weird, tight enthusiasm. Flashbulbs flashed like fireflies. The entry music was "Lord Jesus Come." The eighty thousand Catholics in the stadium sang "Jesus is risen. . . . Jesus is coming!" while the choir responded with "Alleluia!" It was quite a welcome.

Mass began. It was a traditional mass, except Helen Hayes gave the reading from Genesis in a throbbing voice and the intercessions were in several languages.

Whatever one might think about Catholicism, the Catholic mass is splendid. I was gripped by pageantry, by loveliness, by history, and by repetition.

When I studied self-hypnosis in California, we were taught two kinds of trance inductions. A confusion induction went like this: Lie down. Don't cross your arms or feet. Snap the fingers of your right hand. Move your left arm in a circle. Tap your right foot on the floor. Go faster. Now count backward from 100 by threes. 100, 97, 94 . . . Louder. Faster. Louder.

Eventually you snapped into a trance.

A ritual or repetition induction was like this: Lie down. Relax. Don't cross your arms or feet. Empty your mind. Let the tensions leave your body as you exhale. Keep relaxing. Let your eyelids get heavy . . .

The hypnotist would begin to count slowly from one to ten. The spaces between the numbers stretched farther and farther apart. Your body got heavier and heavier. You entered the trance slowly, sinking back through the layers of consciousness to a dark, shining place.

The Catholic mass is a repetition induction. It has been repeated for nearly twenty centuries countless times all over the world. It induces a feeling of timelessness, hence of eternity. Einstein proved that time is actually alterable, but its subjective qualities were already familiar. Within the mind time jerks, hurries, swings, winds slowly. It dilates and contracts. In sleep it disappears.

By the time of the Pope's homily, I was loopy from the droning, the rising and falling of the readings, and the choir singing.

I tried not to slip under. I left the dark Special Lounge and went into the bright empty corridor. *Maybe the Lord does hear the cries of the poor, does give solace, maybe deprivation really is purity, maybe the meek do inherit another kingdom. . . .* I went into the bathroom and washed my face. Soon I went back to my seat.

The Pope's homily was about the beggar Lazarus and the rich man who ignored him, but I was reminded of a story about a different Lazarus. "He is not dead but sleeping," Jesus said, and Lazarus lived again. The Pope's visit had awakened a sleeping dinosaur in the psychic landscape. I could feel the homunculus of this dinosaur clumping around in the more modern parts of my mind. No wonder I felt confused.

This Pope plays to cameras and crowds with immaculate timing. His latest coup has been to cut a record with Infinity, a division of MCA. On *Pope John Paul II Sings at the Festival of Sacrosong*, recorded during his trip to Poland, he offers one of his own compositions, "The Moment of the Entire Life." Infinity has pressed a million copies, so for $9.98 you can have the infallible voice of God's representative on your own turntable.

If John Paul II has modern methods, he does not have

modern views. As somebody must have said by now, man created God in his own image, and the God of our fathers is just that. John Paul II has made it clear that in the Catholic church women are holy breeding stock. He has come forth with equally antiquated views on celibacy for priests, on abortion, on divorce, on birth control, on homosexuality, and on releasing priests from their vows. He does seem to be against violence and poverty.

By the time Communion actually started, I thought my detachment was complete. But it was foolish of me to think I could watch this explicitly holy scene without a lot of mental twitching.

The priests fanned out through the crowd; there was a priest in each section on each level of the stadium. The communicants lined up. Some extended cupped palms to the priests, some took the wafers on their tongues.

I asked the arson squad man what the difference in styles represented. "With your hands you get to feel closer to the Host, you know? It used to be you couldn't touch it. Only the priest could touch it."

Communion seemed to go on and on. I asked my friend if he would do it. "No," he said. "You've got to be in a state of grace and I'm not."

"Are you sorry?"

He didn't answer. We were looking over the railing into the radiant faces of those receiving the body of Christ.

"They're beautiful," I said, wishing I could erase my question. "Look at the light in their eyes."

"When I was a kid," the cop said, "I was afraid for the wafer to touch my teeth. I was afraid it was a sin. Can you imagine?"

"I can imagine," I said. "When I was a kid I thought the

rhythm method was something about how you did it. I thought it sounded like the best way. You know, I got rhy-thm."

We both laughed a long time, but then the laughter got sad.

"Listen," I said, "would it be a terrible sin for me to take Communion?"

His face worked with emotion. "Not for you," he said. "You're not a Catholic. For me it would be a sin."

"Tell me how."

He hesitated, then cupped my hands together. "The priest will say, 'This is the body of Christ,' and you will say, 'Amen.' "

I went to wait behind the priest in the next section. A Secret Service man was standing behind me. I was afraid to get in line. I watched one face after another open itself to the wafer. I began to shake. The Catholic church, like the color white, is a construct to describe the absence of something. I felt an anguish I never expected.

I got my bag, said goodnight to my temporary friend, and left fast. Inside the subway station a teenaged girl was painting, onto the faces on the billboards, fingernail-polish tears of blood.

My eyes ached as if I'd been standing in a glare. I wasn't sure how to assess what I'd seen and felt. Maybe for a few hours in Yankee Stadium a group of the meek inherited the earth. Maybe for a few hours the handicapped were not damaged, but God's special children. If God is a superstition, we live in a time when the word *superstition* no longer seems useful.

The political implications of the Pope's tour frightened me. The energy in Yankee Stadium made the energy that drove the rock concerts and the demonstrations of the sixties seem puny. And in the vivid silence that filled the stadium while the Pope spoke, the rumble of a subway passing made me think of the sound that precedes an avalanche. The church is an institution which predates the secularization of government, and John Paul II has made no comforting statements about the separation of church and state. If the Pope's visit signifies the Second Coming of Christianity, the dinosaur has slouched into Bethlehem to be born.

Middle-aged woman in a New York City ashram: *I do hatha yoga, I raise kundalini, I like chanting, I do the Catholic church sometimes, the Pentecostal sometimes, the Baptists are cool too. I even went to India, and here's what I learned: All those things running up and down your spine, all that light racing inside you, it's all God, even sneezing is God.*

Drunk man at the counter of a breakfast joint: *The Pope spoke to me today, he really did, he came right out of the crowd and shook my hand. He knew my name, he said, "Hello, Nick."*

What Is This
Thing Called?

When I was living in New York, I gave a party to watch Zeffirelli's *Jesus of Nazareth* on television. My friends and I would smoke dope, drink wine, and be smartly detached from an old story. I like junk epics, from *The Poseidon Adventure* to *The Ten Commandments*, and I like retellings. Anyway, Jesus was an interesting man, and he's at least as important as Einstein. My friends thought such a party was sophisticated. However, they did not realize that I intended to watch all three hours of the movie.

During the Resurrection I was sitting by myself in a cloud of reefer. Most of my friends had gone home. A few remained in the kitchen, drinking wine and talking. It was better that I was alone because I was not acting smartly detached. Instead I kept laughing and crying. This behavior did not seem sophisticated, merely weird. David, who used to be my editor, was the last to leave. "It's all right," he said, holding onto my hand. "I like Jesus too."

I am living in my hometown now and I do not hang out with smartly detached friends. Instead I spend lazy days with people who cultivate their pleasures as meticulously as they cultivate their summer vegetable gardens. I find my new friends' lifestyles as exotic as they find my ambitiousness. "Why do you work so hard?" one of them asked me. "I don't know," I said, and stopped. For a while I let my days evolve into explorations of how tan I could get, my evenings into bouts of pinball and pool and disco. If I get any more laidback, I told my new friends, I'll have to be mounted on rollers.

Jesus of Nazareth played on television again. The rerun was an expanded eight-hour version, offered as a mini-series. I didn't give a party to watch it. I cleared my social schedule, stocked my refrigerator, rolled a tiny mountain of joints, and settled in for a week of psychodrama with Jesus. During the second installment, when Jesus talked tenderly to his doubting disciple Thomas, I found myself hallucinating about a woman I used to be in love with. Zeffirelli's Jesus didn't blink. This woman, whose name was Noreen, never seemed to blink either. If the eyes are the windows of the soul, Noreen's could have flown in or out easily. Looking at her eyes, I had the sensation I was falling into them. She made me feel forgiven.

I was in love with Noreen a decade ago, and now I'm not sure what I needed forgiveness for. I do know I'm older than Jesus, and I want to hang it up about Western guilt.

Rebirth is a fashionable notion, so my timing feels right. I can't think of any other concept that would unite Bob Dylan, Jerry Falwell, and Larry Flynt. My concept of rebirth seems more modest than this unusual trinity's. I am not interested in rededicating my life to Christ but in returning to my sources. I spend a lot of time with my mother and sister. Recently my mother gave me a book I'd cared about as a child. I spent several hours reexamining *If Jesus Came to My House.* I like the pictures and the rhymes and the unselfish message, and I like Jesus's little halo. When I look at Jesus's halo, I think about the rosy nimbus that settled inexorably around each of my lovers.

Since I left my husband, I've been in love with several women. The first time I felt a tremendous innocence. I even felt cleansed. I was more sexually aroused than I'd ever been, and I spent several weeks wandering in an erotic haze. I remember walking back to my apartment early one February morning quite dizzy with elation. The snow on the sidewalk was pocked and gritty, and the garbage can by my front door had spilled. The label from a can of green beans blew against my leg. I looked at the trashy street and saw it transformed. The green-beans label against my Levi's was utterly beautiful. I remember thinking, I've never been this happy. I also remember thinking, This must have a price. A few months later—when I was drinking myself dumb and mumbling, I can't live without her—I paid my debts. Not only were my emotions clichéd, they were overwhelming. I felt dreadful and trivialized as well.

The second time I fell in love with a woman I was braced for it. I knew I'd catch it again, like the flu. I moved through my lines with graceful detachment. Not surprisingly, the affair didn't last.

Then I met another woman I couldn't live without. She left her husband, I left my girlfriend, and we moved in together. The magic receded, and I tried frantically to retrieve it. Within a few months I began to stutter. I began to whisper. I had trouble finishing sentences. One day I started to cry in the post office. When this woman left me I took one hundred and five aspirins to soothe my headache, and after I was released from the hospital she hadn't changed her mind.

As the years passed, I met a woman I lived happily with for a long time. I'll never leave you, I kept telling her. Now I know that when I say forever I mean about five years. Our breakup was extremely painful, but I was not suicidal. After all, I wrote to a former professor, how many names can you cry in the night?

After R. and I separated, I concentrated on what I called the Lamaze method of emotional survival: If I breathed evenly enough, pain would simply be another fascinating experience. My libido felt like a marble rattling in a box. I had a few crazed sexual reactions, but I didn't fall in love. Slowly I realized that one reason I had resisted ending the relationship was that I couldn't fool myself into the same groove again. Leaving her would involve the death of something larger than that relationship.

And where would I be without passion? How would I organize my time? I know what I'll do, I'll go back to Charleston. I spoke with my mother, from whom I'd been estranged. Come on home, she said, after all, tomorrow is another day.

So I came home to puzzle over old plantations tucked among housing developments, tunnel-like highways with mossy oaks arched over them, pungent cascades of flowers, ante-bellum neighborhoods—a whole culture of antiques. I often wear a T-shirt that says CHARLESTON CHARLESTON CHARLESTON CHARLESTON. I am so glad to be home that twice I've lain down on the ground and hugged it. My love for home has provided me with a respite from more painful passions. I've had a lot of time to think about my personal life.

The word *passion* originally meant suffering, agony, as of a martyr. The passion of Christ. No wonder being in love made me feel out of control.

Love is an altered state; it changes our vision. I remember the first moment I saw R. transformed. We were sitting on a hillside in Vermont, admiring the landscape. I thought R. was nice-looking, but while we sat on that hillside she took on a certain glow. I could see flecks inside her brown eyes. The freckles on her shoulders looked like gold dust that had scattered from her hair. In that moment R. became numinous for me, and I fell in love. Light settled around her, and she became larger than the natural view.

Looking back, I know it was inevitable that the magical qualities I had experienced would eventually reverse themselves. After R. and I separated, I saw her on the street with a man she briefly married. Her grin seemed to stretch from ear to ear, her jaw thrust harshly forward, and her eyes were too close together. She actually looked demonic.

Recently I spoke to a woman with whom I became friends after R. and I broke up. Linda told me she'd met R. at a party. I was intensely curious. Linda hedged. "It's always odd to meet someone else's obsession." I prodded her and she shrugged. "Well, she seemed like a nice girl to me."

Years ago, my friend David met a European model on Christopher Street. They tricked, and David fell in love. The model returned to Europe. LOVE REAL, the telegram David sent insisted. PLEASE RETURN. He did return, but promptly fell in love with someone else. "You're having a dream," I told David. "This emotion is not authentic." But, when I consider the length of time David's attraction to this man has troubled him, I'm not so sure. David's anguish has grown skin over it; that's all.

It may be dangerous to push metaphor too far, but I think falling in love is the only religious experience my generation legitimizes. We cannot talk about magic or seeing God or believing in astrology without seeming silly. Even those of us who still read the *I Ching* or *Holy Bible* do so surreptitiously. But falling in love is as democratic as puberty: It happens to almost all of us. We can talk about falling in love as seriously as we talk about quantum physics, astronomy, Latin America, or nuclear power. Romantic love is the only mumbo-jumbo we all agree upon.

Before the twentieth century, a lot of songs were about

God. The chief theme of popular music is love, whether we are listening to Patti Smith sing "Gloria," hearing how "Layla" got somebody on his knees, or hanging around "Kingdom Hall" with Van Morrison. The punks insist they only want to be sedated, but Dee Dee Ramone recently got married. In our music the passion of Christ has been replaced by more carnal trials.

I don't know whether I'll fall in love again or not. Right now, I'm busy trying to get reborn. I was once told that people who jump out of windows or off buildings are attempting rebirth. I don't know if this is true, but I'm extremely suggestible, and my notion of rebirth is more eccentric than I like to admit.

Skydivers, after eleven seconds of freefall, reach what is called terminal velocity. One's rate of descent increases for the first ten or eleven seconds, but then the body's resistance to the air stabilizes the rate of falling at about one hundred twenty miles an hour.

In terms of passion, I hope I've achieved terminal velocity. In midair, I feel only my own weight. Einstein once wrote, "There came to me the happiest thought of my life. . . . If one considers an observer in freefall . . . there exists for him during his fall no gravitational field—at least in his immediate vicinity." I don't think we're emotionally constructed to endure the earth moving half a dozen times. Back when covered wagons were fashionable, I doubt if people fell in love over and over. Repetition has destroyed my sense of gravity.

Last week my mother gave me a photograph of her taken when she was sixteen years old. This photograph moved me the way watching Jesus had. I was moved because my mother was once sixteen years old, her mouth was tenderly painted, and she had signed this repossessed gift to an early boyfriend, "With all my love."

Once I went with my friend Penny to see a movie called *Marjoe*. *Marjoe* chronicled the life of a faith healer who had been trained when still a child for religious exploitation. As an adult, he continued manipulating people's religious needs. Then he let some "hip" film makers document the fraudulence behind his ministry and the sincerity of his victims. I knew at the time I would prefer twitching ecstatically on the floor to being one of the film makers or the faith healer. This was not necessarily a moral position. The people transported were having a much better time.

So, when I find myself meditating on the depth and history of clichés, I start thinking, Oh Jesus, I bet I take that love trip again. Luckily, Charleston is locked firmly into my numinosity slot. It is the past that glows in a light I can't quite interpret.

Tough

Blood landed on my lips the first night. The Tough Man Contest had come to Charleston, and these were only the preliminaries. Wright, Mindy, and I were sitting at ringside, right beside the judges. I trusted the ropes after the first few bouts, and when the huge, wet bodies of the fighters fell above me, I didn't bother to turn my head. Wright wiped the blood and sweat off my face. "Jesus," she said, "what's going to happen in the finals?"

In college I studied fiction writing (another dangerous business), and one of my teachers warned me about linear tension: "If the girl is raped with a pistol at the beginning of your story, it'll be hard for the reader to care much when her dead body is gangbanged in chapter five." I took this advice seriously, but the Tough Man Contest was not fiction.

The Tough Man pageants are like beauty contests for men. Any male who weighs over 175 pounds gets a chance to play Rocky for a day. The only restrictions are that entrants pass a medical exam, sign an injury release form, and haven't won a sanctioned amateur boxing match within five years.

Dean Oswald is one of the Tough Man organizers. A sleekly muscled ex-boxer with a gray pointed beard, Oswald told me, "People want to see fights. They want to see crashes. They don't go to car races to see winners, they go to see wrecks. They like to see these big guys punch." He added confidentially, "The American people are very violent." Oswald's voice is rich and persuasive, so he doubles as emcee. When I asked how to spell his name he said, "Oswald as in Oswald."

At least fifty Tough Man competitions have been held in the last year. It doesn't cost anything to enter, but it costs about $10 a ticket to watch. Runners-up get $500, and winners get $1,000.

"I'd fight for that kind of money," Mindy said. Mindy is a television videographer in the daytime. At night she's usually a dance teacher. Mindy, who has the slight build and rapid gestures of the born speedy, went to the Tough Man Contest with Wright and me "just for fun." Wright, a photographer and graphic artist, made a superb copy of her press pass for Mindy. Wright was nervous, so she brought a quart of bourbon in her camera bag. I was nervous, so I brought a few joints. The audience was nearly half women, but we were the only female press.

The first night was a blur of fighting and screaming. The music from *Rocky* played before each bout. Between rounds a pretty girl in a blue bikini walked around the ring holding up a poster that said *one*, *two*, or *three*, depending on the round. Miller beer, the local sponsor, was paying for her services.

The thirty-two contestants wore gloves and mouthpieces, just like real boxers. Over their shorts they wore heavy black leather jock straps, like codpieces, which starkly connected the violence with sex. Each fight was three two-minute rounds.

Wayne Altman, a six-foot-five-inch white man with long hair and a headband reminiscent of flower children, fought a black man named Woodrow Wilson. Wilson, overweight, goateed, afroed, was a foot shorter than Altman. He didn't have much chance, but he kept touching himself on the chest in a go-on-hit-me gesture, even when he seemed barely conscious.

A potbellied disc jockey named Buzz came into the ring wearing an orange cape and prancing like Ali. He picked up the Miller beer girl and swung her around in the air. His opponent was a young black man who quickly bloodied Buzz's nose. Buzz took an eight count, still standing, before the ref stopped the fight. "Why didn't you lay down, Buzz?" Oswald said through the mike, and Buzz flopped dramatically to the canvas. The winner, William Peeler, was trying to look cool, but he was hurt too, and he nearly fell out of the ring.

Two black guys did some real streetfighting, but when one of them got thrown to his knees and covered his head with his gloves, the audience laughed and booed. The other guy jumped flat on top of him. Oswald said whoever was booing should sign up and fight.

Some white men behind me had begun to cheer against blacks. All of the organizers I met were white, but the audience and contestants were about evenly mixed. The drawings for opponents were supposed to be random. However, most of the pairings were black-white.

Mindy kept pouring bourbon. Wright kept taking pictures. I bought some M & Ms that were hot and crushed. A black fighter got knocked out and had to be carried away. A black man in the audience went berserk. A dozen cops converged on him like a pack and dragged him out. Wright whispered to me, "Do you think this eases racial tension or makes it worse?" She looked worried, even scared. "Why are we watching this?"

I was rubbing my thighs while a fist snapped a fighter's head back. "It's a male fantasy."

"We're not males!"

A miserable-looking boy, maybe twelve years old, came over to talk to the judge beside me. "I'm in trouble with Momma, Dad. I been yelling stuff at the Miller girl."

"What kind of stuff?"

"You know. Stuff."

"You ain't in trouble," the judge said. "Go on back to your seat." He turned to me and said cheerfully, "He's been yelling stuff at the Miller girl." He rose and went to talk to Miss Miller, who had put a T-shirt on over her bikini. The next time she walked past the kid she leaned over the ropes and winked heavily at him. Two bright red circles appeared like wax on his cheeks. He squirmed in his chair and hung his head. "Ha, ha, ha," the judge said. "He'll remember *that* for a while."

"*Will the man from the Charleston Police Department, Clay Thornhill, come to ringside!*" Oswald shouted into the mike.

The theme from *Rocky* was nearly drowned out by cheers and boos. "This really is a psychodrama," Wright said. Thornhill was white, and luckily so was his opponent. Thornhill hurt him fast, and at the end of the first round he sat dazed in his corner. Miss Miller walked past him and raised her T-shirt. He came out for round two fighting like a crazy man, and Thornhill quickly knocked him down. At the ten count he hadn't even twitched. When intermission was announced, two doctors were giving him smelling salts and pulling down his codpiece so his crotch could breathe.

Wright and I went outside with the Miller beer girl to smoke joints and drink bourbon. "I'm an unemployed stripper," Miss Miller told us. Her real name was Kim. She used to work in Goose Creek for a woman named Mercy. Kim was sweetly pretty, but her eyes seemed glazed. "I may be arrested for assault. I blacked my boyfriend's eye."

"*Before* you saw this?" Wright said, pulling out the quart. We began to pass it with the reefer.

"I'm pretty fucked up," I said. Then, "Hi," I said to the badge in front of my face.

The plainclothesman was furious. "How could you be so *stupid*? You're fifty feet from the *entrance*, for God's sake! You're standing beside my *car*, for God's sake! Pour it *out*! Put it *out*!"

Wright emptied what was left of the bourbon onto the pavement. Miss Miller stomped on the joint. I showed my own badge. "I'm working too."

We went to look for Mindy. While we were standing among the crowd in front of the main doors, we watched a man walk up behind a friend of his. He laid his hand on the friend's shoulder. "How're you doing?" The friend turned and socked him in the face.

The rest of the fighting that night was unremarkable. Violence may be orgasmic but it peaks hard and fast, becomes jerky, abrupt, and disappointing. When the blood landed on my face I didn't care. I felt the beginnings of revulsion. I had the kind of headache that comes from being hit.

The next morning I tore the door handle off my car. "Must have been loose," I mumbled to my dog. Then I broke an overhead light fixture, trying to kill a fly with a swatter. "I don't believe in this stuff," I told my dog, and drove into town early.

County Hall, where the Tough Man competition was being held, is a cavernous building in an unfashionable area of Charleston. Boxers, wrestlers, and rock stars perform here. An opera singer wouldn't. I parked in the deserted yard. Fiction may be linear, but memory is not. There was something I hadn't wanted to think about last night.

Next door to County Hall is William Enston Homes for the aged. My grandmother lived in one of these ugly Victorian buildings. She lived in the one right next to County Hall. She died there too, when I was twelve years old. My father was with her. He told me once how she had struggled for air, running across the room. He had to hold her down trying to quiet her. He said her fingernails turned blue. A year later my father was killed in a wreck.

After my father's death I wouldn't sleep in the nightgown my grandmother had given me. I wanted to burn it, but I knew that was too violent.

At William Enston Homes, my grandmother had a television to occupy her silence. Her favorite show was *Queen for a Day*. Every afternoon she watched as women told ghastly stories about their lives. The audience applauded to choose the worst story.

After I'd sat in the parking lot awhile, I drove to Wright's for dinner. Mindy had already arrived. Wright's apartment is in a hundred-year-old house in the elegant area called South of Broad.

Several years before Wright was born, her mother lost her right arm. She was riding in a car, and a board protruding from a passing truck caught her elbow. The arm tore off. Wright's childhood was haunted by a clumsy prosthetic device hanging in a closet.

Now Wright's apartment contains two mannequins. Melissa stands by the front door. She wears a tuxedo vest and an antique top hat, but she has no trousers and no arms. Angela is a white wicker torso in the corner. The painted plaster head of a woman rests on the mantel. A deformed doll named Courtney sits in a tiny chair. Wright's stereo speakers rest on Red Cross shipping boxes labeled "Human Blood."

"Violence is the opposite of art," Wright said. We were eating rare steak.

"This is my guess what," I said, holding up a glass of Cabernet. "You just ask Jesus."

Wright had laid a tablecloth, lit candles, and put joints in a silver cigarette case. "A fine dinner is the first defense." She had sautéed fresh spinach "for brute strength, just in case."

"Why do you suppose those guys really want to fight?" I asked.

"Haven't you ever been hit in the face?" Mindy said. "It's a real high." Mindy's hair is curly and sticks straight up, as if she has been shocked. Wright has pale straight hair and pale eyes behind rimless glasses.

"Any way you pass out is a trip," Wright said. "When I was little I used to hyperventilate until I lost consciousness. It was a neighborhood game."

"Were you hit in the face when you were a kid?" I asked. "I never was."

"My parents were both librarians," Wright said. "I was locked in the bathroom when I was five years old for saying a double negative."

Paranoia. Maybe it was from the cheap pint of bourbon we took with us, in case we had to pour it out again. Maybe it was from thinking about my grandmother. Maybe it was the fear of getting busted. Would the same cop be there? See us? Paranoia is the dark sliding and moving, light hurting the brain. "You drive," I said to Mindy. "I'm too busy hanging on."

We arrived at County Hall before the fights started. The crowd was about the same size. Maybe a thousand, maybe twelve hundred. Roughly half black, half white. More than a third women.

Carl Jung speculated that consciousness began as a response to violence. Maybe someone killed a beloved brother or son, and when the rage was over, the loved one was still dead. At any rate, according to Jung, human consciousness is "a recent acquisition of nature. . . . It is frail, and easily injured."

My vision seemed flat, as if my depth perception were gone. The crowd was quieter, but appeared to bulge in places. "Have you read Jung?" I asked Mindy. We had taken our seats right under the ropes. Wright was wandering with her camera.

"Nope. Never will, either." She was grinning at me.

I thought of history accelerating, one long act contracting toward a single point. Sixteen fights the first night. Now eight more. Then four. Then two. Then one. Apocalyptic release. Orgasm. Death. Winners. Wright once said to me, "The hardest things to understand are right in front of us. Like sex. Like sleep."

I must have looked weird because Mindy put her hand on my arm and said, "Want to hear a bad joke? You look pretty rocky."

Oswald began to boom through the mike, telling the rules, hyping the crowd. Then he told everyone to stand for the National Anthem. We stood, but there was no music. "The tape is broken," Oswald said. "I can't sing, so let's get on with the fights. We'll bring on the anthem later."

The theme from *Rocky* played while the sixteen remaining fighters ran single file around the hall, like horses on display. I saw one fighter go find his girlfriend in the crowd. He touched her as if he were knocking on wood.

Wright came back to her seat.

"This is like a group psychosis," I said.

Wright shrugged happily. "Pain is pleasure, or everybody wouldn't be having such a good time."

A cornerman was struggling to pull the heavy jock strap over the shorts of an overweight man. "It won't hurt nothing? You sure?"

"You gotta have it, you gotta have it."

His opponent was a bald white guy, at forty-eight the oldest man fighting.

The bell rang. The old guy, Giordano, scored fast with a left. The referee laughed with delight.

"Hit him, Pop," someone yelled.

Boxing, it can be argued, is an art. It is at least a sport. Giordano brought dignity into the ring, but the Tough Man Contest was not sport. It was theatre. "Everybody would like to beat the hell out of somebody," one of the organizers had said to me. Gloves may protect the hands but they also blunt blows. Leather protects the crotch. The idea of violence without consequences is thrilling. In California, in the sixties, when humanistic psychology was the vogue, I knew several people who owned boffers. Boffers were sponge-rubber swords you could clobber people with without damaging them.

I realized Wright was the person yelling, "Hit him, Pop!"

Mindy leaned across her and handed me a Coke with bourbon. She stage-whispered, "Reminds me of an acting class I was in. All the boys wanted to play Jesus."

"This is great tonight!" Wright clubbed me on the shoulder. "I'm not a bit scared!"

"Maybe violence is a path of knowledge," I whispered to Mindy. Wright was getting tired of us talking across her. She separated us as if she were a referee. "Back off, ladies."

In the second round Giordano was tiring. His opponent crouched and waved his gloves, but he was no match for the older man. Giordano looked grim, stony. The crowd loved Giordano, who at the final bell smiled like a delighted kid and hugged the black man as intensely as a lover. Two blonde teenage girls were standing near Giordano's corner while his victory was announced. One of them was crying. They were both wearing green T-shirts that said MY PAPA, THE CHAMP.

In the next fight Wayne Altman went up against a man with coppery skin and a heroic body. Both men seemed to know what they were doing in a ring, but Altman had about five inches on his opponent and maybe twenty-five pounds.

Altman's nose began to bleed in the first round. By the second it seemed to have swollen shut. In order to breathe, he had to suck hard around his mouthpiece. His mouth expanded and contracted in an awful rhythm while blood ran from his mustache.

"That white guy's demo'd," Wright said when the fight was over. She pointed at the tube that ran from the basin the fighters spit into. The bottom curve of the plastic tube was dark pink with blood. "And they use the same mouthpiece over and over," Wright said. "I've been watching."

"It's gotta be white!" I heard someone yell. "It better be white!" The cornerman dropped bloody adhesive tape onto my notebook. I threw it at Mindy. "Souvenir!"

"Great! I'll put it with my collection of used condoms!"

Altman won on a split decision.

"The white guys are ahead!" the voice behind me shouted.

During intermission, I insisted we walk to the car to smoke a joint. We were parked far down the street, in front of a supermarket. My paranoia had eased, but I was still jumpy.

We turned on the radio and air conditioner and I tried to relax. "I feel like I'm getting half the facts wrong," I said.

"Maybe accuracy is overrated," Mindy said.

Wright held up the bourbon. "Here's to telling the story, not the way it happened, but the way it should be remembered."

"Hey, that's not bad," Mindy said.

I wanted to tell them about my grandmother. I wanted to tell them how earlier that day the past had torn the present like paper. Instead I said I was nauseated, which was true.

Too much time had gone by. I was afraid we'd miss Giordano in his next fight, so I insisted we trot back to County Hall, instead of walking. When we reached the paved parking lot we could hear wild cheering. We broke into a run. I was ahead of Wright and Mindy, so I only saw what happened out of the corner of my eye. Wright stumbled, tripped, and skidded on the pavement. I heard the pint break.

I thought she'd hop right back up but she didn't. She was curled on her side like a caterpillar.

"Good thing I've got the camera," Mindy said, extending her hand.

"Let me stay here a minute." I didn't like the look on Wright's face, so I picked up the camera bag she'd been carrying and gingerly turned it inside out. The film canisters were wet but sealed. I shook the dripping pieces of glass onto the ground. "We sure do lose a lot of whiskey."

Wright was sitting up. One elbow was scraped, the knee of her jeans was torn, and her palms were bleeding.

"Audience participation," Mindy said.

"Wright's got stigmata," I said.

"I don't think this is very funny," Wright said.

While Wright went to the bathroom to wash off the blood and grime, Mindy and I went back to our seats. When Wright came back, her eyes had a hard, inward look.

I told her Giordano didn't want to fight again, and that the cheering we'd heard had been for a knockout. She didn't answer. "Are you really okay?" She didn't answer again.

One of the organizers, a wiry, skinny man, tapped me on the shoulder. "Would you girls be willing to lead the crowd in the National Anthem?" he asked. "None of us can sing."

Wright turned her camera toward him like a weapon.

"I guess we don't know the words," Mindy said.

"I guess we can't sing either," I said. "Even if we are girls."

The rounds after intermission were disappointing. A lot of people had been injured or had withdrawn. Only two things happened that I thought were significant. The first was that, during the next to the last match, Wright screamed, "Nuke the Iranians! Kill Picasso!" The second was that, while everybody who'd won at least one fight came into the ring to receive a tinny little trophy, Mindy went to the microphone and led the crowd, a cappella, in "The Star-Spangled Banner." She shook her ass and jabbed her finger at the sky like a rock star.

Later, in the parking lot, I gagged, then gagged again.

"Gonna throw up?" Mindy asked cheerfully.

I shook my head. "Did you know my grandmother died in that building? Right there?"

Wright put her arm around me, to steady me. "Don't worry," she said. "It'll go away. It's only the present, and it's almost over."

"I know," I said. "I'm just knocked out."

Ambush

November 3, 1979, 11:20 a.m. The Communist Workers Party's "Death to the Klan" rally in Greensboro, North Carolina, is scheduled to begin at noon.

A caravan of eight or nine vehicles containing Ku Klux Klansmen and Nazis pulls slowly past the demonstrators gathering at Morningside Homes, a predominantly black housing project. No police are present, claiming confusion about the parade's starting point. Four television stations and the Greensboro *Daily News* are not confused, so videotapes and eyewitnesses record the following scene:

The morning is clear, blue, and vigorous. Uniformed Communist children chant around an effigy of a Klansman. Some twenty-five Communists and Communist sympathizers hand out leaflets and talk with community people. The crowd numbers about one hundred. Spirits are high, even combative.

As the cars creep down Everitt Street, chants of "Death to the Klan" begin. Taunts, threats, and obscenities break out. Some of the marchers hit some of the Klan cars with sticks.

The first car stops near the front edge of the crowd. The last of the caravan stretches behind the intersection. Now the only avenue of retreat for the demonstrators is up Carver, a shallow street more like an alley. Near the front of the caravan, someone fires a gun into the air. Fistfighting, then more shooting starts. The marchers stampede toward the narrow mouth of Carver Street.

When the first shots are fired, men lumber out of the last two cars in the caravan, a yellow van and a white Ford sedan. Someone opens the trunk of the Ford. The sixteen-year-old head of the Nazi Youth Corps begins to distribute an arsenal of shotguns, rifles, pistols, even a semi-automatic M-15. Half a dozen Klansmen and Nazis stand in the middle of Everitt Street and methodically begin to shoot people.

Cesar Cauce charges the gunmen with only a picket sign in his hand. He is hit in the chest and head.

Bill Sampson is carrying a .38, although the Communists have agreed to the city's demand that they be unarmed. Sampson takes cover, begins to return fire. He is hit in the heart, and throws his gun to Rand Manzella. Sampson's last words are "Keep on shooting."

Mike Nathan, a doctor, goes to aid Sampson. Nathan is shot in the head.

Sandy Smith takes cover behind the brick corner of the building. When she sticks her head partway out to see what's happening, she is hit between the eyes. "Call a doctor," Sandy starts whispering. "Call a doctor." She dies crouched on her knees, leaning against a wall.

James Waller, a doctor, is dying a few yards away from her. Waller had been part of the medical team at Wounded Knee.

The gunfire stops. It's quiet now, except for screaming. The Klansmen and Nazis calmly put their guns away. The man firing the M-15 never drops the lit cigarette from his mouth. The caravan moves on.

The police miraculously appear, but every vehicle except the yellow van escapes. They quickly arrest a dozen Klansmen and Nazis, but it's too late to prevent a historically important event: Armed conflict between two organized political groups has broken out in North Carolina. Its form has been a slaughter. The lawn at the corner of Everitt and Carver streets is a battlefield scattered with bodies—four dead, one dying, ten wounded.

Sally Bermanzohn is dazed. She rolls Cesar Cauce over, as if she expects him to wake up from playing dead. "Oh, my God, help us!" she shouts, but there is still denial in her next words: "We need an ambulance!" She finds her husband, Paul. He is alive but critically wounded, shot in the brain.

Signe Waller and Dale Sampson are still behind cover, protecting a group of children. "We've got to see," Dale says. She finds her husband, Bill, lying dead on the grass in Carver Street.

James Waller sprawls nearby. Nelson Johnson, the only black male and the only North Carolina native among the Communist leaders at the rally, is trying to tend to him. Johnson listens to Waller's last labored breaths, watches his eyes glaze over. "He's gone, Signe," Johnson says. Waller, the highest-ranking Communist on the scene, has been shot in the back.

Riot-control police appear. They train their guns on the gathering crowd. Someone yells, "The fucking bourgeoisie did this!" A woman leans into an abandoned but still running video camera. She talks wildly about armed self-defense. A white male reporter is pressing his palms together, pacing up and down. "What can I do? What can I do?"

A black woman approaches a white cop crouched behind a car. "Why did you shoot these people?" The cop looks scared. "I didn't shoot anybody, lady." A tense cop cocks his shotgun at the crowd. "It was a miracle he didn't fire," the reporter who saw this told me.

Rand Manzella is in shock. He is still clutching the pistol Bill Sampson tossed him, and his photo is taken both kneeling and standing over the body of Cesar Cauce. These photographs add to the impression that both sides in the fighting were significantly armed.

Nelson Johnson is talking to a mostly black crowd on the sidewalk. Johnson tells them that the Klan is a tool of the ruling class. He says the Klan divides whites from blacks so they won't fight their real enemies, the capitalists. "We declare war on the capitalist system!"

Johnson is arrested for inciting to riot. He resists, and the cops stomp his hands. He's already been stabbed in the arm. Willena Cannon, a black Communist sympathizer, tries to aid Johnson. She is arrested too.

Rand Manzella is arrested for walking around with that pistol. Manzella is charged with being "armed to the terror of the people," an old statute generally used to control the Klan.

Signe Waller sits on the ground beside her dead husband. The cops keep trying to make her move. A video camera focuses on her grieving face. "Long live the Communist Workers Party!" She raises her fist. "Long live the working class!"

When I asked Signe Waller what field her Ph.D. was in, she said, "I don't remember." I pressed. "Okay, philosophy of science. But I work in a factory now, or I did until they fired me. They've fired a lot of us. Look, it doesn't matter what class we're *from*. What matters is whose class interests we *serve*."

Signe, who is forty-one years old, has a placid face with high cheekbones and direct, brooding eyes. When I suggested that the Klan and Nazis accused of the murders, some of whom can't read or write, many of whom were factory workers, might represent the working class as accurately as she could, she scoffed. "They're scum. Goon squads. Shock troops."

I asked why so many of the Communists I'd been interviewing spoke in jargon. She smiled almost shyly. "I'm not sure. It's a question we ask ourselves a lot."

Followers of the Communist Workers Party describe themselves as sympathizers, supporters, workers, or friends. Actual party members are an elite. Their number is secret, but has been estimated at less than a couple of hundred, a fact that has contributed to the dismissal of them as a lunatic fringe group. Followers view membership as an honor. "It's only for the very best of us," Signe said, trying to explain the secondary role she played. Her husband, James, had been a member of the CWP's Central Committee, presumably its ruling body. "I don't *aspire* to membership," a white man working in the CWP's Break the Chains Bookstore in Durham told me. "It may *happen*." He had a loaded pistol on the desk beside him.

The CWP originated in New York's Chinatown in the early seventies. It was known then as the Asian Study Group. Around 1973 the Asian Study Group became the Workers Viewpoint Organization. Only a month prior to the November killings, the Workers Viewpoint Organization renamed itself the Communist Workers Party.

The CWP "line" includes unqualified admiration for Chairman Mao, qualified support for Pol Pot, and enthusiasm for the Zimbabwe and Iranian revolutions. Members like to talk about the objective laws of history and the science of MLMTT, Marxism-Leninism-Mao-Tse-Tung Thought. They call each other comrade. They see feminism as bourgeois trickery, homosexuality as sickness, and revolution as necessary surgery on the social structure.

The Communists lead rigidly normal lives. Marriage is correct, children are correct, hard work is admirable. Drugs and unsanctioned sex are decadent. They live in unpretentious houses in unpretentious neighborhoods. They try not to make too much money.

The roots of the Communist Workers Party are in the sixties. At the heart of the CWP are radicals who never drifted into the hedonism and political repudiations of the Me Decade. If their visible progress during the seventies was slight, wheel spinning only increased the depth of their commitment. The Communist Workers Party members and their disciples believe with messianic certainty that they will lead a revolution in this country.

The group murdered on November 3 were highly educated and had substantial radical histories. Four had worked openly as Communist union organizers, three at Cone Mills.

Since party members are required to "join the working class," James Waller, who was thirty-seven at the time of his death, worked in a sanitation plant. Before that, he worked at Cone's Granite Finishing Plant in Haw River. During Waller's two years at Haw River, union membership rose from some fifteen members to nearly two hundred, out of a work force of seven or eight hundred. Waller led an explosive strike at Haw River, and was running for president of his local when Cone fired him for falsifying his job application—he hadn't mentioned being a medical doctor. Then the parent union, the Amalgamated Clothing & Textile Workers Union, shoved five Cone locals into receivership. This meant that elections were suspended, and the local union representatives appointed from above. Waller's charisma and effectiveness are clear: Despite the fact that he'd been fired and the elections declared illegal, his local met and elected him president.

If Waller had turned away from practicing medicine for money, he had not turned away from using his training. Often, at night, his kitchen was like a clinic. When patients were too poor, Waller paid for the medicines himself.

Michael Nathan was the only Communist killed who was not actually a party member. However, Nathan's devotion to the CWP was unquestionable, and he was inducted into the party in his hospital room before his death. He had never regained consciousness.

Nathan, thirty-two, was chief of pediatrics at Durham's Lincoln Community Health Center, a federally funded clinic which serves a predominantly black and low-income population. He also held a faculty appointment at Duke Medical School.

A working-class kid from Washington, D.C., Nathan had been involved in radical causes since his undergraduate days at Duke. When the maids and cafeteria workers struck, Nathan was part of the group who occupied the president's office. His social conscience took his medical skills to Guatemala. "All he wanted to do was help people," his wife, Marty, told me. Marty Nathan is also a doctor. "When I first met Mike," Marty said, "I told him I was thinking of going to South America to practice. Mike said he knew how I felt, he'd tried that alternative himself. He said he found out he could help the people in South America more by staying here and working for a Communist revolution. That really turned my head around."

Cesar Cauce, twenty-five, was born in Cuba. His father was in Batista's cabinet. Although his family fled communism in Cuba, Cauce embraced it here. After graduating magna cum laude from Duke, Cauce worked as a data terminal operator at Duke Hospital. He edited the union organizing-drive newsletter, and he once co-led a delegation of Duke workers to Washington to demand that the American Federation of State, County, and Municipal Employees try harder at Duke.

Floris Cauce has told of finding her husband on November 3. First she tried to stop Nathan's bleeding. "I put my hands over the holes in his head, but they were too big. Blood kept coming through my fingers. Then I thought, Where's my husband? I saw him on the ground, and someone was sitting there holding his hand. He was unarmed when they killed him. They shot him again while he was on the ground." She added, "My husband was one hell of a fighter. He was a most uncompromising man."

Bill Sampson saw his first cross-burning as a child growing up in Camden, South Carolina. A physically beautiful and sensitive man, Sampson was brilliant and popular in college. By his senior year at Augustana College in Illinois, he'd won many honors—Phi Beta Kappa, president of the student body, and a scholarship to spend his junior year at the Sorbonne. The 1968 student revolt in Paris changed him, and when he returned from France he led Augustana's first demonstration. It was certainly nonviolent—the college president's wife even served cookies to the protesters.

Sampson went to Harvard Divinity School for an M.A., then moved on to medical school at the University of Virginia. There his patients included brown-lung victims from the textile mills. Just before Bill would have graduated, he quit medical school and went to work in a textile mill, as a union organizer. At Cone's White Oak plant in Greensboro, Sampson was a shop steward and was running for president when the locals were put into receivership. He was thirty-one when he died.

Sandy Smith, twenty-eight, was the only black and the only woman killed. Like Sampson, Smith grew up in South Carolina. After graduating from Bennett College in Greensboro, where she was a civil rights activist and president of the student body, Sandy stayed in town. For five years she worked at Cone's oddly named Revolution plant. Revolution had no union, so Sandy led ROC, the Revolution Organizing Committee, a group that functioned as a de facto local, filing grievances, fighting unfair firings, and agitating about safety conditions at the mill. A newspaper columnist named Ted Magnum, who'd known Sandy since college, remembered her as intense, dedicated, and full of love. "The irony of the whole insane, murderous incident was that she cared so much about unnecessary human suffering; she probably cared more about the conditions of the man who killed her than human hatred will allow him to see."

The day of the Communists' funeral was cold and rainy. The National Guard had been called out, and the nine hundred Guardsmen, highway patrolmen, and Greensboro cops far outnumbered the four hundred mourners. The coffins were draped in red and rolled through the streets of Greensboro to public Maplewood Cemetery, where no whites had been buried before. Signe Waller and Dale Sampson carried unloaded rifles as part of an honor guard. Signe marched at the head of the procession. In a curiously reasoned and openly anti-Communist article in *Harper's*, poet Robert Watson described Signe as a person "who some feel is one of the most militant and belligerent of the group," and mocked her march in front of her husband's coffin. "Signe Waller in the vanguard looked like a female Ernest Hemingway on safari." According to Signe and Nelson Johnson, Watson failed to interview any of the Communists present at the killings.

The Communists claim to have been strengthened by the deaths on November 3. Certainly their resolve has not wavered, and nationally they've gotten a lot of publicity. But the leadership in the Greensboro-Durham area was nearly wiped out. My delvings in North Carolina turned up only seven people who were unequivocal CWP leaders. Waller, Sampson, Smith, and Cauce were killed. Paul Bermanzohn, another doctor, nearly died. Charles Finch was not present. Nelson Johnson was arrested immediately, and in the media the deaths of his friends were more or less blamed on him. "Violence Not New to Leader of Rally," an article on the front page of the Greensboro *Daily News* asserted the day after the killings. "His presence at the Saturday violence marked the second time in ten years Johnson has been a leader in activity that brought death, destruction, and injury."

Nelson Johnson is a soft-spoken, compelling man. In 1960, while he was vice-president of the student body at North Carolina Agricultural and Technical College, a teenager he'd been tutoring ran for president of a local high school. When the student, Claude Barnes, was declared ineligible for the election, students wrote in his name and he won by a three-to-one margin. In the ensuing conflict, the administration suspended a large group. The teenagers went en masse to the college looking for Nelson. The police arrived, the students rioted, and a nineteen-year-old black man was shot and killed. The National Guard swept the campus. Nelson was arrested for creating a disturbance. He went to prison. His sentence was commuted by the governor at the request of an impressive collection of black leaders. Banker B. J. Battle has said, "Nelson was one of the few people in Greensboro who could rally black people across the spectrum. He has been consistent in working for the down-and-out. People trust him."

Nelson Johnson walked me around Everitt and Carver streets, quietly re-creating the scene. He's not sure why they didn't kill him on November 3. Maybe it was the beret he was wearing, maybe they were avoiding killing black men on purpose, maybe they were afraid that if he died the black community would burn Greensboro down. Johnson is certain the CWP was set up, its leaders targeted and assassinated. "It was a basic military maneuver. These were SWAT-type assassins."

The CWP had applied for a parade permit for their demonstration on Friday, October 19. The police stipulated that the marchers be unarmed—no large sticks for the picket signs, no guns. The CWP is known to advocate "armed self-defense," but Nelson wondered why the cops kept bringing up weapons. "Are *you* expecting violence?" Nelson says he asked. "It was a heavy lesson. We made a complete and total mistake. They kept insisting how they would protect us, so we thought the cops were planning on violence, that if there was going to be trouble it would be because they would plant a provocateur or something. We had a whole piece of thinking on how to deal with that. And it was eerie, you know, when we got here. After all this discussion, where were the pigs?"

The pigs were at the wrong location. The only exception was Detective Jerry Cooper, who had followed the Klan-Nazi caravan to the killings.

The parade permit, which the police themselves had issued, stated that the demonstration would begin at Everitt and Carver streets at noon. The Communists knew they were vulnerable at the beginning of the march, while their leaders were gathering and the crowd wasn't large. As a security measure, all publicity said the march would assemble at 11 a.m. at Windsor Community Center, some three-quarters of a mile from the real location. This way, only the police and the marchers would know where the leaders were, and the Communists would have an hour's leeway to unite the two groups.

On November 1, the day the permit was granted and two days before the rally, Nelson Johnson and Paul Bermanzohn held a press conference. A man named Dawson told Paul and Nelson that he was an unhappy worker. He talked with Nelson awhile. When the Communists had gone, Dawson went into the police station, identified himself as a Klansman, and asked for a copy of the parade permit. The police gave it to him. Now three groups knew the real location of the march: the Klan, the CWP, and the cops.

Then, according to a ninety-two-page report that Chief of Police A. E. Swing issued to justify the cops' absence on November 3, they started reading the Communists' publicity instead of their permit. The police decided the parade might begin at Windsor Center. One assumes they didn't read carefully enough to notice that the Windsor Center starting time had been moved up to 11 a.m. Otherwise they wouldn't have scheduled the police escort to arrive at 11:30 a.m., or sent the TAC squad out to get sandwiches during the crucial half hour.

In his report, Chief Swing admits the cops had an informer in the Klan-Nazi group. Detective Cooper was the source of this information. The cops knew that the Klan and Nazis were assembling at a house on Randleman Road in Greensboro. They knew that the Klansmen were armed at least with handguns, and that they planned to follow the route of the march. When I asked Chief Swing why the police didn't bother to notify the CWP that a Klansman had the permit, he told me they didn't think it was important.

At 11:06 a.m., Detective Jerry Cooper located the Klan-Nazi caravan parked on a ramp of Interstate 85. At 11:13, he followed the caravan to the rally. If other cops were confused about the rally's location, Cooper was not. At 11:22 police radio transcripts quote him: "They're now at the formation point."

Cooper, who could see the fighting from where he stood, appears to have been a bit slow in calling for help. The firing went on for several minutes before other police arrived. The killers even had time to reload. Later Cooper tried to stop two television cameramen from filming Nelson Johnson's arrest.

I asked Nelson Johnson if he thinks the whole police department was involved in the conspiracy he insists was behind the killings. "Oh, no, it wouldn't take more than two or three to manipulate the situation."

Johnson admits he has no basis, other than political analysis, for asserting that the FBI was involved in a plot against the

CWP leaders. However, later in my research, I did find evidence that might support FBI involvement.

Andrew Pelczar is the field agent for the FBI in Greensboro. Immediately after the killings, Pelczar gave interviews to the Charlotte *Observer* and the Durham *Sun*. These interviews quote him directly about an FBI investigation of the CWP in Greensboro-Durham which began on October 23, 1979. "Andrew Pelczar . . . said the investigation was started because of the organization's frequent statements supporting 'the use of violence to achieve its goals.' While Pelczar would reveal little of the FBI's preliminary findings, he did say the group was active in the Durham area, had some out-of-state ties, and might be linked with an unnamed Greensboro business."

Pelczar said "no comment" when I read him these quotes. His superiors in the state and national FBI offices flatly denied that the FBI had investigated the CWP before November 3.

Obviously, prior investigation of the CWP does not connect the FBI to the killings, but the dates of the supposed investigation are disturbing. The Greensboro *Daily News* reported that the FBI investigation was completed on November 2, the day before the killings. If the investigation was begun on October 23 and completed on November 2, this would mean that the FBI studied the CWP in the Greensboro-Durham area during a brief period that fits neatly between the date the Communists applied for their permit, Friday, October 19, and the date on which five of their leaders were killed, Saturday, November 3.

Nelson Johnson believes there must have been a state intelligence source identifying the Communist leaders. It does seem remarkable that gunmen could fire into a crowd of one hundred people, kill four of six leaders present and fatally wound a fifth, without knowing who the individuals were. Everyone was hit in the head or heart, and they were killed either with buckshot, which is ballistically nearly impossible to identify, or with rifle bullets which passed through the victims' bodies. Since the district attorney has dropped all conspiracy charges against the Klansmen and Nazis, it is now necessary to prove who shot whom. Acquittals seem possible.

"Go look at some of those videos," Nelson said. "Then tell me it wasn't a military maneuver. Tell me they didn't fire a signal shot from the lead car and stampede the crowd toward the killers. Tell me it wasn't a planned ambush."

I'd already seen the extraordinary videotapes two newsmen from Durham's Channel 11 made on November 3. I'd slowed the film down, run it over and over, discussed it with reporter Matt Sinclair, who'd been handling the sound equipment. I wish my impressions weren't so similar to Nelson Johnson's.

Later, when I spoke with D.A. Mike Schlosser, he argued against a pattern to the killings. He suggested Nelson Johnson, Signe Waller, Dale Sampson, Dori Blitz, and Rand Manzella as other possible leaders. I pointed out that, of these, only Johnson was even a party member. Schlosser didn't think the fact that all five were hit in the head or heart suggested sharpshooting. "When you shoot, you shoot to kill." When I asked Schlosser about dropping the conspiracy charges, he said, "Conspiracy is hard to prove. Where is the evidence of conspiracy?"

I told Schlosser how uncomfortable I'd been, watching the Channel 11 videos. I remarked about how calm several of the Klansmen and Nazis seemed, unworried about returned fire or fire from behind them, that is, from the police. Schlosser must have misunderstood what I meant to imply, because he said, "Oh, yes, it was like a turkey shoot."

When I was at Everitt and Carver with Nelson Johnson, he said, "You know who'll probably end up going to jail because of all this, don't you?" He smiled slightly and touched himself on the chest. "They need to discredit me."

. . .

The first confrontation between the Communist Workers Party and the Ku Klux Klan in North Carolina had occurred four months earlier. On July 8, in a small town called China Grove, the Federated Knights of the KKK showed *The Birth of a Nation*. The Communists organized a counter-demonstration. Two Confederate flags belonging to the KKK were burned. Joe Grady, who'd been one of the leaders of the Federated Knights, was at China Grove. He told me that both sides had been armed and that preventing violence was difficult. Some of his men had to be restrained physically. Grady warned his troops that if shooting began the three policemen trying to maintain order would be killed. The KKK, of course, is against killing policemen.

According to the Anti-Defamation League of B'nai B'rith, which monitors the Klan, Klan membership died down during the early seventies. Now the Klan is on the rise again. National membership has increased by 50 percent since 1975.

Six factions of the Klan vie for support in North Carolina. Joe Grady and Gorrell Pierce had led the Federated Knights, but after China Grove, Grady charged Pierce with Nazi sympathies and split off to form the White Knights of Liberty.

The most militant of the Klan groups is led by Virgil Griffin, and centers around the small western North Carolina towns of Lincolnton and Stanley. Glenda Thompson of Stanley proudly told the Charlotte *Observer*, "If you don't want to run into a Klan member in Stanley, then you better watch out where you buy your cigarettes, your groceries, your gas, and your insurance, who writes up your speeding ticket, and which plant you apply for a job at."

The Klan's humiliation at China Grove was bitter. If Gorrell Pierce began to flirt with the Nazis, Griffin took more decisive action. He allied his group, the Invisible Knights of the KKK, with the Nazis and the National States Rights Party. The new alliance was called the United Racist Front.

Griffin admits he helped organize the Klan-Nazi caravan. He told me he was at the November 3 rally. Another Klan source placed him in the lead car.

At a Klan meeting that preceded the November killings by only a few weeks, the Charlotte *Observer* reported that Griffin said, "If you cared about your children you'd go out and kill 100 niggers and leave them dead in the streets." After November 3, Griffin told the *Observer*, "The Communist Party has always been our main goal. . . . If there was no Communist Party, there would be no problem with niggers."

The FBI questioned Griffin for a few hours about the shootings, then released him. He has since been arrested for cross burning.

The Communists had no notion that the China Grove confrontation was causing splits or increasing militancy in the KKK. They were delighted with China Grove: no violence, media visibility, and a bravely anti-racist image. They wanted to take on the Klan again. The Klan reverted to holding their rallies in secret. The CWP decided to try to bring the Klan to them. Nelson Johnson wrote a public letter to "Joe Grady, Gorrell Pierce, and all KKK members and sympathizers" challenging them to show up at the "Death to the Klan" rally. "The KKK is one of the most treacherous scum elements produced by the dying system of capitalism," Johnson wrote. "But, as we showed in China Grove, the Klan is a bunch of cowards. . . . The Klan will be smashed physically. . . . We take you seriously and we will show you no mercy."

"What did you expect, with a letter like that?" I asked Johnson. "Didn't you expect some kind of violence?"

Johnson shook his head. "We had taken some security measures, but both Pierce and Grady had said in interviews that they definitely would not show up. We didn't know about Griffin. Look, I told you we were worried about the cops. The Klan really are cowards. The idea that the Klan are this awesome force, to be feared, that shit has to be gotten over. To ride up and shoot unarmed people has got nothing to do with *brave*. The Klan wasn't capable of planning this thing. The state planned it."

"A lot of people think *you* provoked the violence."

Johnson shook his head again. "It's true we believe that revolution is inevitable. But there is no way you can take a military initiative if the people are politically disoriented and confused. This is our line, and this was our line that day: military defense, political offense. We believe in armed self-defense. That's just, you know, sensible. But our main tasks are obviously political. We were offensing the Klan politically. We were not offensing them militarily. That's why we agreed to disarm for the march. Bill Sampson had his .38 because his life had been threatened a bunch of times. Somebody had a Derringer. You don't think we'd be seriously armed with a .38 and a Derringer, do you?"

I'd checked lots of eyewitnesses to find out if the Communists had more arms than pistols. Everyone said no except for Chief Swing, who had not been present. "Swing said you had shotguns."

"That's a total lie. Look, the military thing is pretty new to us. We don't have a lot of background. Or equipment. The Klan had the element of surprise. We were just . . . out of position. They knew we weren't armed. It was a costly lesson."

I recalled my initial impression, gleaned from reading press accounts, that these were armchair Marxists who'd had a brutal brush with reality. "Well, it made you look naïve."

"It'll take some time to overcome that. People would have respected the party more if we'd wasted four or five of them too. This stuff is not on the campus anymore."

. . .

The last night I spent in Greensboro, I dreamed about Signe Waller and woke up screaming. Like many people who were more or less radicalized by the turbulence of the sixties, I drifted away from politics in the seventies. I stopped talking about social justice and capitalism, good guys and bad guys, and started focusing on moral complexities and ambiguities. The feminist notion that you must work from your own oppression soon became, for me, an excuse for an entirely personal approach to life. I liked to quote Pogo: "We has met the enemy, and it is us."

In Greensboro, I spent dozens of hours interviewing CWP members and followers. I talked with the chief of police, the district attorney, Klan leaders, eyewitnesses, and reporters who'd written about November 3. Later I read hundreds of press accounts, searching for evidence, contradictions, or patterns. I studied the CWP's journal and newspapers. I talked to the FBI, both local and national, and to the Justice Department. I even took the police department's self-evaluation and radio transcripts and set up a map of Greensboro, charting where various policemen were during the killings.

Greensboro became an obsession. I spent four months writing drafts that were intensely different from each other. I was torn by questions of language, questions of interpretation. If I called the Communists unified, was that different from calling them ingrown? Is a man armed only with a picket sign who charges half a dozen gunmen a hero or a fool? Doesn't the word *fanatical* describe the same quality as the word *dedicated*? And what does it signify, on the eve of the eighties, for a man with a Harvard divinity degree to die saying, "Keep on shooting"?

Like many who've written about November 3, part of me wants to blame the victims: *You asked for it, baiting the Klan. They kicked your asses good. Don't challenge power. Don't trigger the right wing. Be quiet. Find a personal solution.*

The dedication and physical courage of the Communists I

met in North Carolina frightened me. When I interviewed Paul Bermanzohn in his hospital room, his hair was growing jaggedly in, but did not cover the deep groove the bullet had made. I watched him trying to walk down the hospital hall-way. This thirty-yard journey would take him ten minutes. "They can kill every one of us, and it won't matter. If we fall, a wave of others will take our places."

Even Chief Swing seemed unnerved by the Communists. "Listen, you've talked with these people. What kind of woman sits by her husband's body and says, 'Long live the Communist Workers Party'?"

The Communist Workers Party members and sympathizers I met in North Carolina are as ruthless and selfless as a re-ligious sect. For them, jargon is holy. "You don't know what we've been through," Sally Bermanzohn said. "We *need* the sense of history in those words. I like being called comrade." The fact that the Communists are willing to die has led many people to think that they want to die. People who will lay down their lives like offerings on the doorstep of history can generate a lot of power. I keep trying to understand if violence can be an act of love.

I don't trust "armed self-defense." After all, that's the Pentagon's position too. In "politically offensing" the Klan, the Communists have repeatedly published a photograph of a Klansman in his robes kneeling over the body of another Klansman. The caption reads "A racist snake gets his." This photograph looks depressingly like the one of Rand Manzella kneeling over the body of Cesar Cauce. I doubt that the good ole boys of the Klan are capable of nice intellectual distinc-tions. To them, "death to the Klan" is the same as "death to the Klansman." Regardless of whether there were trained assassins in the caravan, interviews with Klansmen have made it clear that most of them thought they were going to a good head bashing, to prove their courage. One car contained seven dozen eggs for heckling. In their jail cells, before they were released on bail, the Klansmen and Nazis sang "Onward, Christian Soldiers."

The Communists don't admit that they're trying to start war in North Carolina. However, they believe revolution in America is essential, and it's only a short leap from that position to trying to start armed conflict. This does not, of course, mean that they tried to trigger their own ambush.

Whether the Communist strategy in North Carolina is inadvertent or deliberate, it is shrewd. The Ku Klux Klan is an existing, armed right-wing militia, and in North Carolina it's legal to carry guns. By challenging the Klan, the Communists place the state's military forces in a difficult position. The police and National Guard must either side with the Klan or defend the Communists. Twice since November 3 the National Guard has been called out in Greensboro.

A lot of people in Greensboro seem afraid. The white waitress in my hotel's coffeeshop said, "Nobody comes downtown since the trouble. When I saw those bodies on the TV, I said, Oh lordy, I hope my boys aren't mixed up in that mess."

The black waitress looked up sharply. "On whose side?"

An eyewitness newsman who was pulled off the Greensboro story, he's not sure why, took me into a private room and closed the door. Recently he saw another reporter who'd been present November 3. The reporter pretended not to know him. "People are scared. Nobody knows what the hell is happening. Listen, I don't want to die on some dark road one night just because a lot of right wingers have gone crazy."

Before I went to Greensboro, I took firearms lessons. I told my editors that since guns were so important in understanding what's happening in North Carolina, I wanted to remember how handling them felt. Looking back, I think I was acting on instinct. Bob Dylan once wrote, about a different decade, "You don't need a weatherman to know which way the wind blows."

Partying Is
Such Sweet Sorrow

I went to the 1980 Democratic Convention with a central question: Who are these people and why are they acting like this? Mainstream politicians seem airbrushed, and looking for individuals among them borders on a contradiction. That's why I decided to follow my home state's delegation. As my sister once put it, Southerners act just like other people, only more so.

Monday night. I sat in the lobby bar of Manhattan's Summit Hotel, where half a dozen small delegations were shuttered. The crowd was jubilant. Kennedy had just lost the rules fight and with it the nomination. I turned to a woman sitting nearby. "I'm looking for some real people. I don't suppose you're from South Carolina."

She was the lieutenant governor. Nancy Stevenson is a divorced woman with a colorful past. Before her entry into politics she co-authored two successful mystery novels. She also collaborated on a third novel which has been attacked as prurient: *Savage Summer*. Nancy Stevenson has smart, ironic eyes. In her stylish white suit, with her hair neatly knotted, she managed to look both unpretentious and elegant. Her "Democrats Do It Better" button hung from her lapel like old jewelry. As we discussed her novels, I wondered if her sense of irony was inbred. Her pseudonym for the mysteries had been Daria Macomber. "As in 'The Short Happy Life of . . . ,' you know?" She looked pleased but surprised that I did. The pen name for *Savage Summer* was changed because "we had fans for the first two books, and this one was . . . so different."

I began to loosen up. The man standing beside Nancy said, "They have more policemen in New York than we have people in our town!" But he was sure Gaffney mattered. "Within a fifty-mile radius, we have more than a million people!"

A woman alternate pulled me aside to whisper doubts about Nancy Stevenson. Nancy, she claimed, is a political threat to the governor. "Governor Riley is the hub of our wheel. He's real. When our New York hostess said, 'I don't know whether to call you Dick or governor or what,' he said, 'You can just call me your highness.' He has arthritis. That's why he can't turn his head."

A delegate named Mary Michaels told me how she got elected. "I chose the reddest, reddest, reddest dress I could find, and I just blinded them." Mary, who seemed bold and personable, wore a bright red dress with a dramatic white shoulder. Mary is a high school English teacher. Teachers were the largest profession represented at this first Democratic convention half composed of women.

Mary wanted to make sure I knew which of the Carolinas she was from. "I met this lady in the bathroom, I meet a lot of people in bathrooms, and she said, Aren't you from North Carolina? I told her I may live near the border, but

I certainly don't consider myself a North Carolinian." She looked at me meaningfully. "I *adore* politics. AP, UPI . . . everybody really wanted to know what I thought. I felt downright important. It was beautiful."

Sitting beside Mary was a reporter from Spartanburg. He had a non-Southern look, and I learned he was originally from Long Island. He'd lived in South Carolina for twenty-five years, but natives are born, not made. "I like it down there because it's personal. You can call the governor Dick. See that guy over there at the bar? He's a state senator, and he's Jewish, which is unusual for South Carolina, and he's just a regular guy."

Nancy Stevenson stepped over to say goodnight. She had to be at the *Today* show very early, so she was going to skip dinner and "pig out on Godiva chocolates."

Flora Condon, an alternate, came through the lobby doors. Earlier Flora had told me, "I'm a party party party person. I don't smoke, I don't take more than a cocktail or two, but I can go into a crowd and it stands my hair up. You're a part of making history!"

I sat in the Summit lobby for two more hours, but my sense of individuals was already blurred. Fifty people in the delegation, three thousand delegates, two hundred million Americans. I began to grasp the obvious: One problem in politics is multiplicity.

The next morning I called Communist Workers Party headquarters. I thought the CWP might be planning disruption. Since I'd interviewed some of them in Greensboro, they'd staged simultaneous demonstrations in eleven cities, hit John Anderson with an egg, and been arrested several times for interrupting the trial of six Klansmen and Nazis accused of murdering some of their leaders. Two of the Communist widows, Floris Cauce and Marty Nathan, were in jail for contempt. During the trial Marty's mouth had once been forced shut with adhesive tape.

The press officer for the CWP informed me that the other two widows, Signe Waller and Dale Sampson, were in New York. I wanted to see them but no longer believed the CWP would manage to cause trouble. Security at Madison Square Garden was thorough, the Democrats had gripped my attention, and Signe and Dale were receding as personalities. I chased them to one press conference, missed them, and gave up.

Sallie Peake and Mary Ward hadn't been friends before the convention, but they were tight with each other now. I met them at the South Carolina morning caucus. Sallie, a tall black woman, was wearing a black suit. Mary, a wiry white woman, was wearing a white dress. "I am *not* a schoolteacher," Sallie said. "You do *not* have to be a schoolteacher to be in politics."

"These teachers resent people like me," Mary said. "They're angry that a person who is not a professional could be a delegate. I'll tell you, though. I never dreamed that a textile worker could come to a national convention. I'm a textile worker and Sallie works in a factory too."

Sallie said, "Some people think they're better than us because we sweat for a living. I could have had an office job, been somebody's secretary, but it wouldn't pay my bills. I've got four children. We earn more than those teachers, and we can dress better too."

"I've been in politics since before I was old enough to register," Mary said. "I went to stump meetings with my daddy, and I've been active in the union for years."

"I serve people, not color," Sallie said. "That's why I don't attend the black caucus and don't belong to the NAACP."

"The day's going to come," Mary said, "when your color and my color will be the same."

The beer-chugging contest at the Summit took place a few hours after Teddy Kennedy's concession speech. When I arrived in the lobby, a lot of people were already drunk. A sign said "Equal Rights for Apes."

A sleazy young man put his arm suggestively around me. He told me he was only twenty-three years old and he was vice-chairman of the delegation. When I asked how he'd gotten such a position, he boomed in my ear, "I campaigned like hell!" Then he told me his father had been in the state legislature, and his cousin was married to the daughter of the chairman. In politics the line between nepotism and inheritance is delicate.

I went into the bar, where the competing delegations were beginning to organize. The six states staying at the Summit were South Carolina, Alabama, Mississippi, South Dakota, Hawaii, and Idaho. Each group would have a chugging team of four members. The hotel had bought T-shirts with the state names on them, and several delegations had brought their large posters from the Garden.

Deena, a chimpanzee, was going to judge. Deena was wearing Levi's and a Levi jacket. She was introduced as president of the Texas Chili Association. Someone handed me a bumper sticker that said "Deena Does Dallas," with "Rent-a-Chimp" and a phone number printed in small letters. I liked Deena. She looked intelligent and relaxed.

I watched a pretty delegate in a red suit. She grinned continually, perhaps thinking this would prevent anyone from noticing a short blond guy who was massaging her breast.

"Alabama'll win," a handsome man in a camel's-hair suit said to me. "Why, we had to pick and choose to get the best drinkers."

Behind me was an older woman with a wrinkled tan. She was part of the Alabama cheering section and wore a black T-shirt that said "I Have No Drinking Problem / I drink, I get drunk, I fall down / No problem."

The announcer said Hawaii was passing up the competition; they must be busy eating macadamia nuts.

An older man climbed onto the stage and began to lead Alabama football cheers. "We're gonna raise some mortal hell!" the man in the camel's-hair suit said.

I was leaning across a woman trying to eat shish kebab. "I'm only from Oregon," someone at her table said.

"Don't you dare step on my shoe again," a middle-aged lady behind me threatened.

I saw McKinley Washington, a black minister and the only Kennedy delegate from South Carolina, sitting quietly in a booth trying to finish a hamburger. People were standing all over his seat.

In the first round Mississippi whipped Alabama because the third Alabama drinker put his glass down with some beer left in it. Apparently Deena was a sharp-eyed judge.

Next South Carolina went against Idaho. The four S.C. delegates lined up across a table from the four Idaho men. The signal was given and they began to drink frantically. Beer dripped out of the eyes of the first Idaho chugger. Everyone was shouting and waving signs.

"Screw Idaho!" someone behind me yelled. I turned. The screamer was a red-haired man in a gray three-piece suit. He was standing on a table.

A man in a green blazer yelled, "Everybody must get stoned!"

The South Carolina team finished first, but they were disqualified because one chugger, Duby Thomson, poured most of his beer down his face instead of swallowing it. A woman said, "South Carolina's been beaten by the damn Yankees again!"

South Dakota had a separate round by themselves, competing against the clock. When they were through, the announcer said, "South Dakota may have the only girl contestant, but they sure can't drink beer!" The finalists would be Mississippi and Idaho. "Okay," the announcer said, "go back in the bathroom and vomit. Stick your fingers down your throats and be back in ten minutes."

I returned to the lobby. The members of the South Carolina team were falling against each other and shrieking. A black man with gray hair said to me, "Duby's tight! If he had taken his teeth out, we'd have won! His teeth slipped into the glass!"

I didn't stay to see Idaho win.

New York was full of expensive parties during convention time. I took a cab to the Empire State Building. The bash for a congressional candidate was nearly over, but a tired man with a scarred invitation list waved me through. I took the express elevator to the top and went straight to the bar. A man in an ape suit was standing beside me, but nothing surprised me any more.

Soon I was sitting on the observation deck. The only other time I'd been on top of the Empire State Building was on my high school senior trip, when the tourists were herded around in packs. Now I was nearly alone, and I felt a splendid isolation. I leaned against the parapet, looking up at the red glowing spire. Birds circled it like motes of dust in light.

A guard asked me if I was all right. I nodded yes and walked slowly around the deck. From this lofty point I could see all of Manhattan, and farther too. Gold arteries of light ran toward the World Trade Center, the rivers wound serenely around the island, and it all looked clean and artistic. Politics, I kept thinking, is about distance. The politician tries to fit the person to the pattern. Linking the personal and the political is like trying to combine sex with math. Perhaps this can be done, but how?

Soon I found myself sitting on the floor again. The man in the ape suit sat beside me as if we were old friends. His ape head was tucked under his arm, and his naked face, thrust through the hairy neck of the suit, seemed fragile.

A black man who said he was a politician from New Jersey sat down on my left.

"This is all so strange," the man in the ape suit said.

"Eight million people are too many," I said.

"For a party?"

"For a city."

The black politician said, "I know a lot of guys from Russia, and they're not Communists. Just because you happen to be a Soviet, you gotta be a Communist? No way."

I put on the ape's head and looked up. The high glowing spire was blurred without my glasses, and my face got hot fast. "We're in the belly of the beast."

The black man's mournful voice mocked mine: "Sweet girl, sweet girl. This is not the belly."

I went to hear Carter's acceptance speech out of duty and boredom. Firecrackers went off as Carter began to speak, and Secret Service men ran toward an area near the podium. I didn't realize that the woman who set them off was Signe Waller.

A woman jumped up on a press table and began to shout. I couldn't make out her words, and she was tackled by a Secret Service agent. It never occurred to me that the tiny figure on the horizon of the Garden was Dale Sampson.

I settled down to find out whether a winner's speech could be as graceful as the loser's. It wasn't. The enthusiasm, even among Carter's most ardent fans, was forced. Watching the demonstration was like seeing the Democratic party jerk off. They couldn't even get the balloons on the ceiling to cut loose.

I straggled back to the Summit, where I sat in the lobby, listening to conversations and taking notes. I was thinking about going back to my own hotel to get some sleep when Allen Taylor, a television reporter from Columbia, South Carolina, came hurrying through the lobby doors. "Did you hear what happened with the Communists?"

My mind snapped open. "Those firecrackers?"

"No, outside. There was a fight between a Communist group and the police. A lot of people got hurt."

Taylor told me he'd been in the Felt Forum, near the main press entrance, when about a dozen policemen ran by. He ran after them. While he was outside, the Secret Service sealed the Garden for two hours, from about 9:50 to 11:50. "They said it was because there were too many people in the Garden. But they wouldn't let anybody *in* or *out*. After a while they did start to let people leave, but there were about three hundred media people locked out. Some of them had to go on live at eleven o'clock and they couldn't get back in. You should have heard it. A group of media people chanting, '*Open convention, open convention.*'"

I raced to the phone banks and called the Communist Workers Party press office. Signe Waller had been arrested for disturbing the peace and was now at Central Booking. Dale Sampson had gotten away. The big news was this: Several hundred CWP supporters, wearing helmets and carrying sticks, had marched on Madison Square Garden. In a confrontation with police, twenty-one cops had been injured, seventeen Communists arrested.

About 2:30 in the morning I arrived at CWP headquarters in Chinatown. Unlike the Summit lobby, the Communist office was tense and silent. As at the Summit, the walls were covered with political posters. Signe Waller had just been released, but she was still wearing her delegate disguise: heavy black glasses, a matronly flowered skirt, her hair in a bun. The only flaws in her image were new white tennis shoes, presumably for running, and a lost earring. "I lost an earring? Take those pictures over! They released me on my own recognizance. They said, with my political views, they know I'll be back for my hearing."

When I asked why they had wanted to disrupt the convention, Signe said, "We want the government to know that we will *haunt* them for the murders of our husbands. We *will* overthrow them."

Why firecrackers?

The press officer said, "We want them to know that, with our organization and leadership, we can penetrate into the innermost sanctums of the ruling class. We *can* overthrow them."

I was surprised that two well-known radicals had broken the heavy security at the Garden, especially carrying firecrackers. Firecrackers contain gunpowder. Theoretically, the Communists could have taken gunpowder into the Garden in small amounts and constructed a bomb.

Later it would strike me as strange that Signe was released without having to post bail. It would strike me as strange that Dale, who held a press conference a dozen yards from where she was knocked down, was not arrested. Later I would wonder if Kennedy's awkwardness and tardiness on the podium, his stiff face and brief appearance, weren't related to the trouble with the Communists. The fighting outside started after Carter had begun to talk, so Carter had no way to know what was happening, but Kennedy must have known, and maybe he had the sense to be scared.

Later it would strike me as strange that *The New York Times* didn't report the confrontation with the Communists at the Garden and that the story disappeared from the New York *Post* after one day. Isn't the fact that twenty-one police-men were injured in a confrontation with American Com-munists at the 1980 Democratic Convention *news*? Is it inno-cent to ask *what's going on?*

But riding home from Chinatown at four in the morning, I felt sad and bitter about the Communists. To march on the convention wearing helmets and carrying sticks is not defen-sible as self-defense.

Communism, like New York City, looks best from above. Communist theory sounds like a secularization of Christianity, but Communist practice is often crude and bloody. The Com-munists I've met are manipulated by threads of their own jargon. Lines are by definition thin. I think the Communist failure at language signifies a larger failure of thought.

To believe in a vanguard is to view history as a knife. To believe you are part of that vanguard is to see yourself as the blade. This kind of thinking inspires courage. Signe told me she does not find her bravery remarkable because she takes her guidance from the party. All groups are seductive, and I told Signe how much I would like to belong—to the Com-munists or the Christians or the Democrats or a sorority or even to A.A. I would love to submit, to say, *You tell me.* But history's edge is jagged, its point obscure. The Communists believe that the American working class is going to rise up and follow them. This view is breathtakingly naïve.

The simple and simple-minded are unfortunately similar. Signe Waller and Dale Sampson have something of the heroic about them, but they have reduced themselves to slogans, positions, and aggression with a vehemence the Democrats will never match.

Political cronies and political cadres can't mix, so this story has no resolution. Signe Waller told me the new American revolution will occur within twenty years. A balding lady at the Summit said, "I like this New York life. I'm going home and open my tiny town twenty-four hours a day." And a barrel-chested man put his sausagelike arm across my shoulders. "Say this in your article, honey. Business got done, and a good time was had by all."

South Carolina

When I was fifteen, I killed a black man on Yonges Island, South Carolina. He was lying in the road, drunk, late at night. I was not even driving the car, my friend Marla was.

The man was tangled under the left front wheel. The car was in the ditch. I twisted my ankle getting out of the car. I could see the man in the light from Harry's car, behind us. Harry shouted not to look, but I stooped down beside the black man. There was a lot to say, but I couldn't think of it till lately.

Now I say, Are you dead? I say, Please don't be dead, I don't want you to be dead. Please. I say, Go away, go away, go away. I say, Get out from under the car. What were you doing lying in the road? What kind of crazy thing was this to do?

Each time I say this the black man opens his eyes. He says, Get off me, get your big ugly self off me. You're hurting me. He says, You're cold and white, baby, and you weigh too goddamn much.

The black man says he can't breathe. He has a wife and three children. He says please, his chest hurts, he can't last much longer.

Then she shoves against the car, which has pinned his chest to the pavement. Okay, get off me, you motherfucker, you're killing me. He pushes at the weight crushing his heart and ribs.

He stops and laughs. I was just lying in the road. What the hell did you run over me for? Can't a man even lie in the road?

He fights again. Okay, crush me, I don't care. It hurts too much anyway, I just as soon die. I want to get it over with. I can't breathe. Please let me die.

The car's headlights slice the country dark. Now the car begins to talk. Hey, friend, you're stopping me. Get out from under me.

The black man doesn't answer.

Get out from under my wheel. What kind of asshole would lie down in the middle of the road? You're a crazy nigger and you're jamming my progress.

The black man opens his eyes. Well, he didn't mean to jam nobody's progress, he was just lying in the road taking a little rest. It's a fine thing if you can't even lie down to rest without some goddamn two-thousand-pounder laying down on top of you.

Well, look now, it's over. I'm very sorry. But I can't seem to move with you under my wheel.

I don't seem to be able to move much either. It's a little late, but you should be the one to move.

You don't understand. You are under my wheel, caught in my axle. I am, you understand, trapped here.

The black man says nothing.

I'm trying to be patient with you. Think of my wheel as an arm, my motor as my chest. You are like a knife in me and I can't move. I hate to mention it, but you hurt.

The black man says nothing.

I've been trying not to let you know, but I can't breathe either.

The black man says nothing.

The car begins to cry. Please. I'm trapped here. I can't move. You're a knife. I couldn't stop. I wasn't going fast.

The car begins to gag. The car begins to choke. Its eyes still slice the sky. Somebody put me here, somebody put you there. I didn't mean to do this. I didn't do this myself. Please, it hurts, it hurts.

I have been running up and down that asphalt road for twenty years, between the car in the ditch and Harry's car. I am screaming Harry's name but I don't know why, since he's as scared as I am. For twenty years Marla has been sitting behind the wheel of the car in the ditch, saying Hail Marys. I can only hail Harry, who can't help, and kneel beside the man, who is dead.

I see the man often, in the streets, in my dreams. He holds a silver knife. He says he'll kill me if he can.

Growing Up
Racist

Like every white American I've ever encountered, I am a racist. During the sixties I disavowed and tried to disown racism. Many young whites took up this cause. Yankee students came South on the summer vacations to convince the dispossessed to register. White Southerners like me turned against their families. Some risked or lost their lives. All I chanced was my heritage.

It was a self-righteous, emotional time. I remember telling my mother how I hated her mink coat and hearselike Continental. She was a benevolent capitalist, I sneered, "the most dangerous kind."

I told her that with every step she took she crushed the bones of black slaves. If blacks were too poor to eat correctly, it was our fault, wasn't it? If they didn't have jobs, we were to blame, weren't we? Our forebears had caused this mess, hadn't they? My mother thought I was a young fool and let me go.

I left for fifteen years. Now, when I sit on my rooftop in the evenings, I can see my mother's condominium across the Cooper River. Every Wednesday night I have dinner with my mother and sister at a country club which has never had a black member. After dinner we all play bingo. I have no mink coat or Continental and I still wear jeans, but I do have a nice car, a credit card, and a bank loan.

Racism. The word keeps banging against my mind. What happened to my overriding guilt, my historical understanding, my social conscience? What the hell happened to me?

My racism may be the passive, complicitous kind—I perpetuate the institutions which hold discrimination in place—but active, conscious racism is now widespread. Some black leaders suspect a conspiracy. They cite the Buffalo and Atlanta murders, the shooting of Vernon Jordan, and the acquittal of Nazis and Klansmen in Greensboro. During the Liberty City riots, many newspapers called attention to a certain fact: Rioters had learned since the sixties, and didn't burn small neighborhood-owned businesses. It's a small step to think next of burning someone else's neighborhood. No one wants to talk about what that's called.

The first Civil War began here in Charleston. The South is the only part of America that's been invaded and defeated, and racism is one of our scars. Current racism extends beyond the polarities of North/South and black/white. In San Diego, armed right-wing groups patrol the border searching for "illegal aliens," the Haitian boat people are rejected, Cuban refugees are held in camps, and Vietnamese immigrants are treated with guilt and dismay. In the American melting pot, white remains the only well-blended color.

Willie, the black carpenter repairing my roof, said, "We not talking civil war this time round. We talking race war."

I was shocked, it showed, and Willie gave me the sweetest smile, insisting he hadn't said what I thought.

Interracial social contact is rare in Charleston, and Willie is one of my few black acquaintances. Sometimes we sit on the roof together and smoke reefer. Willie tells me wild stories about how, after Vietnam, he and his brother traveled up and down the East Coast robbing 7-11s and filling stations, doing drugs. Willie became a carpenter because he was good at it, and what if an American made him fire that gun?

Willie likes hearing how I got arrested in a Stop the Government demonstration in Washington ten years ago. While some cops made me lie face down in the grass, I slipped my Swiss Army knife out of my pocket so I wouldn't be charged with carrying arms. I was certain I was a radical, and I had a vague ambition to slash some tires. I was charged with blocking traffic. I don't volunteer that what I miss about the knife is the corkscrew.

"You said race war, Willie. Did you know that lots of right-wing fringe groups are arming? They think race war is coming. They think the Communists will force it."

Willie has elegant hands and a rough, emotional face. "Blacks ain't been armed since the Panthers. We know who offed them, don't we?"

It was probably racist to assume a small-town carpenter wouldn't know about the government's questionable role in the deaths of Fred Hampton, Viola Liuzzo, and the four little black girls killed when a church was bombed in Birmingham. About their campaign against Martin Luther King.

Willie looked at me and winked. "Want to hear a big word I knows? Gen-o-cide."

Well-intentioned white people are often afraid to confront the possibility that they're racists. Scapegoating of Southerners is as common as it is comfortable, and if you're white, you may think my tale has nothing to do with you. If you're not, I think you'll recognize Willie's wisdom: "White people is all the same story."

I grew up inside the right wing. When I was in high school I believed we should bomb the Russians first. I thought fluoride was a Communist plot. Strom Thurmond and Barry Goldwater were my heroes. As president of the student body, I was sent by my high school to a three-day anti-Communist seminar where General Mark Clark was the keynote speaker. All students were required to read J. Edgar Hoover's *Masters of Deceit*. I spent a lot of afternoons worrying about how, when the holocaust with the Russians started, I would manage to save my large, chaotic family.

The Freedom Rides frightened me. I'd read enough comic books to know heroes when I saw them. I watched a busload of Riders on TV with a childhood buddy. I was thinking, Oh, Jesus, what if the Yankees are right? My pal was purple. "Kill the niggers!" Cords of hate stood out on his neck.

I don't remember my family being virulently prejudiced, although several of them told racist jokes. Who, then, when I was a child, taught me not to say mister or sir to black men? Who taught me blacks were descended from apes and had a different smell? Who taught me they were better athletes, more sexual, less capable of distinguishing right from wrong, and dangerous out of their place? Perhaps I merely breathed these lessons in the American air.

When I was in the tenth grade, two other girls and I were riding home from a dance in a deserted rural area late at night. We ran over a black man and killed him. He was lying in our lane. The headlights of another car blinded my best friend, who was driving. I was dozing and awoke to see a body rushing under our wheels.

My friends began to pray. I jumped out of the car to look

at the man jammed into the axle. Blood ran from his mouth and ear.

A white teenage boy and his parents happened along behind us. They helped my friends out of the car, telling them not to look. I was still crouched by the dead man. *Don't look? This has happened and don't look?*

I got into the other car to wait for the police. Our car lights lit the death scene yellowishly. Someone had covered the man's head, but it would take a tow truck to lift the car.

The police and coroner didn't arrive for an hour. During that time, blacks gathered around the body, weeping and screaming. In the ghostly light I could see fifty, sixty, maybe a hundred. I had never heard anything like their sound. "Will they lynch us?"

"No, honey," one of the adults said.

I grew braver. "It's just niggers, isn't it?"

When no one answered, I whispered, "I hate niggers."

The police arrived, joking to ease our fear. My friend's father arrived, told her he would buy her a new car so she wouldn't see this one again.

The next day I found that I could see the crowd gathered round the car and the man's bleeding face whether I had my eyes closed or not. My sense of momentum was distorted, and my car, on curves, tried to separate into vectors. I could hardly breathe.

I am ignorant, I kept thinking. *Flat ignorant*. History had cut a hole in a white girl's mind, and everything I believed was rushing out. Maybe we'd been wrong in the Civil War. Maybe the Russians were nice. Maybe Southerners were monsters.

Inside my memory, scar tissue grew over this event. The wreck receded into paranoia, became an anonymous black man with a silver knife who invaded my dark red dreams, chasing me. I finished high school quietly editing the yearbook, no longer sure why I skipped the eleventh grade to hurry, or why I now loathed home.

I thought I went North to school. I went to Duke, where I placed into advanced calculus and physics. I had never heard of calculus, and the theory of relativity frightened me because it made me think of my relatives. I barely passed English.

My sophomore year I went to see the dean drunk. "Why don't you quit school and get married?" she said.

I got married. My husband was a Southern man who had already conquered the North by graduating high in his class from MIT. He took me to Boston for a year. The hallucinations that had battered me since the accident stopped. Strangers no longer reached out of mirrors. Beams of light no longer came out of my eyes. I no longer sat in a car that wouldn't start while the black man cracked my windshield with his knife.

We moved to southern California and I went back to school. I found out that Keynesian economics had superseded Adam Smith. I found out that Eleanor Roosevelt wasn't funny. I found out about astronomy. I began to write fiction. Only fiction, where I could tell the truth without remembering it, relieved the pressure in my brain.

Stanford gave my husband and me grants, and we moved to Palo Alto for graduate school. Every California apartment we lived in had white walls, white wall-to-wall carpet, and white drapes. I needed the absence of a past. In California I thought I had stopped being white because I no longer noticed it. Almost everyone in my classes and neighborhood was white.

Lots of people move to California to get over having a past. It's our Western myth. But for me California signaled the end of escape.

Encounter groups had become fashionable. My personal life was too quiet. I picked up the Free University's catalog as if it were a ouija board and my planchette finger slid to "Encounter Group in Racism."

For dinner before the first meeting, I'd promised my husband down-home food, fried chicken and Kentucky Wonder beans. He came home to find me sitting silently beside a raw, dismembered bird.

The encounter group was all white, except for one of the leaders. "This is your first lesson," he said. "These groups are for white people. Black folks are busy surviving. I'm your token, your white nigger. I've got a Ph.D. and I can talk white or black. Now let's find out why you're here."

I began to cry with my first sentence. The startled group listened while I stumbled through the shock of reading Malcolm X. Malcolm X was right about white people and Vietnam. On some level I didn't think it was as serious to kill yellow or black people as it was to kill whites. I was horrified by the Nazi slaughter of the Jews, whom I could conceive of as individuals, less so by the American destruction of Vietnamese. How could I change? Atone? I never told this group about the high school wreck because I literally could not remember it.

That came later, in Gestalt therapy. By this time I was wearing Levi's, declaring feminism, and going to demonstrations against the war.

The Gestalt leader wanted to work on my asthma. I lay down on the floor and he put his full weight onto my chest. In a few strange seconds I became the black man under the car. "Get off me!" I started screaming. "White man! Asshole! Honky!" The shouting went on quite a while, but my breathing was worse than ever. This was the most painful hallucination I've ever had. Finally I could only cry and wheeze.

"We're not through," the leader said. "Now, you be the car. Put all your weight onto my chest."

I was afraid. As I lowered onto him, the car's headlights

came out of my eyes. "I can't move myself," I sobbed down at him. "I can't get off you. I didn't mean to do this. I don't want to be here, I don't want to be here!"

My breathing eased as I cried, exploring the fantasies of being the bumper, the headlights, the road, and the weeping crowd. I saw down the tunnel of my imagination. I saw how trauma bruises the whole mind.

Walking out of the group, the only other Southerner said to me, "Listen, that was brave as hell. But I wouldn't talk about it. These white people out here, they think they're racially liberated. I mean, nobody's gonna lay down in front of their cars, you get me?"

After six years of encounter groups, graduate school, people who said Om and starved macrobiotically, I began to dislike California. It had soured like my marriage, like milk. Lack of history made palpable. Altamont. Hell's Angels. Bobby Kennedy assassinated. Ronald Reagan. Doctor Hippocrates, who answered weird sexual questions in the *Berkeley Barb*. Cannibals in Yosemite who carried fingers in their pockets for snacks. A boy who roasted his girlfriend's parents in a state park barbecue pit. By the time I left, I knew some white middle-class professionals who spent a whole weekend in a swimming pool with the temperature set at 98.6 while they drank LSD-improved milk out of baby bottles and rocked each other for comfort. Across the Bay, in Oakland, the Panthers were organizing and arming.

White California culture, I announced, lacked politics. When I left my husband, I moved to a commune in Vermont to be radical.

There were four communes in our vicinity. At one the women wore long skirts and baked bread on a wood stove. The men farmed and made maple syrup. No indoor plumbing, no electricity. Next door was a group of rich kids who sat around writing novels, developing meaningful pictures in their darkroom, and making dance tapes on their electronic equipment. A few miles distant was a group who thought of themselves as politically superior. They were convinced the revolution would begin in Vermont and practiced with firearms in their pasture.

I moved in with a group of disaffected leftish intellectuals. We sat in our homemade sauna, took psychedelics, and had endless house meetings to "confront" each other.

Everyone in each of these groups was white. Soon I found out that almost everyone in Vermont was white. After getting arrested in that demonstration and having some "revolutionary" sexual experiences, I began to dislike Vermont too. Vermont, I said, looked like picture postcards for more than visual reasons.

I moved to New York, where life would be "more real." Within two years there had been three muggings in my elevator, all black or Hispanic against white. An old lady with her jaw broken for $5. It was more real.

For a while I stayed political. I was committed to the women's movement, which I noticed was as racist as California humanists and Vermont radicals.

In feminist groups whites constantly assumed they were the leaders and that black women's experiences of sexual discrimination coincided with theirs. Black feminists tended to identify with and sympathize with their men, which was a source of irritation. White feminists didn't want to hear they might be victimizers as well as victims. If they had to understand the privileged position their whiteness put them in, they might have to start understanding the position men were in with women.

I worked within a deliberately integrated collective named Sagaris. With the National Black Feminist Organization we set up a weekend workshop on racism in the women's movement. This emotionally exhausting workshop convinced me we were trying to move a mountain with teaspoons. White women seemed a swamp of ugly, hidden impulses. I couldn't stop being white, so I stopped being political.

In New York I had one close nonwhite friend. Both of Maureen's parents were doctors, and she'd been married to a diplomat. "Africans are not backward," she told me. "They are different." She repeated *different* in case I was too dumb to understand.

Most of the parties I went to in New York were like my own: a token black or two let us feel superior to overt racists, but provided no contact with black culture. Maureen's parties reversed this pattern. Her Riverside Drive apartment was dominated by African art and extraordinary paintings of black people turning into skeletons. Maureen's record collection made me realize how white my own was. The professionals who hung around Maureen's parties were standoffish with me. If Maureen said I was okay I was okay, but I sensed discomfort, and I felt nervous to be such an outsider.

Maureen laughed when I told her this. "Now you know how blacks feel all the time *if* they make it in the white world."

"Maureen, why shouldn't our cultures be different? Our histories are. Ethnicity is important."

"Ethnicity isn't the problem. The problem is systematic privilege and systematic discrimination."

Later, I found her distinction difficult. How can I embrace my past without embracing the rights and luxuries that come with it? I still don't know the answer.

But, after a few years of New York life, I had a typical dual focus: career and money. My personal life was fragile. For most New Yorkers the family structure, if present at all, is weakly nuclear. I began to long for the dozens of relatives I had once described as an octopus squirming across the state of South Carolina.

Then my white friend Michele was mugged. When I visited her after she got out of the hospital, her face was a dark rainbow of bruises. Her arm was in a cast.

Michele is an English professor. "I was raised to believe racism is wrong, and now I'm afraid of black people. I see a black face and I feel like prey. Every black face looks alike to me. I don't understand what's happened inside me."

Racism for Michele had conjured images of redneck sheriffs with cattle prods and hoses, tobacco-chewing greasers in pickups with shotguns beside them and Confederate flags hanging from their CB antennas. Racism for Michele meant ignorance, not self-knowledge.

Violence pulls the lies off people. As the economic noose has tightened on New York and other cities, the squeeze has of course been worst for the poorest. But when Michele made black people the bogeyman, she made herself into something awful too. Violence is an escalation of what she called *otherness*.

I told Michele that if I were black and had grown up in the South Bronx or Harlem white people might not look much like individuals. Michele said, "So fucking what?" Now she carries a tear-gas gun.

I lived on the Upper West Side. There were welfare hotels around, but cops too. I paid $10 a month to a block association to help finance a private guard at night, but, like John Lennon, I felt safe in New York. If poverty made people vicious, it didn't make them weird.

Then the state began relocating mental patients into my neighborhood. I saw a guy wrapped in plastic with a lampshade on his head, pushing an empty grocery cart. A woman about my age walked my street daily, still in her hospital clothes, old menstrual blood all over her skirt. A block from me a man from a mental ward poured gasoline on a woman he didn't know and set her on fire.

So I came home, where violence is common but personal, and racists know what they are. I would be different. I had learned too much not to be.

In *Understanding Media*, Marshall McLuhan wrote about "the retribalization of the world" through electronics. I came home to rejoin my tribe. I was welcome, despite my radical past and permanent eccentricities. My family were as right wing as ever, but we shared what we have in common: blood identity and a rich connection with place. I had two years of sea breezes, palmetto trees, and folks whose faces, gestures, laughter, and style of storytelling mirrored my own. Happiness came to me like a package lost in the mail.

Then, in the 1980 elections, my cousin Glenn ran against a black man for the state senate. If Glenn won he would be the first Republican from the Charleston area since Reconstruction. If Bill Saunders won he would be the first black.

Glenn, who used to be a Legal Aid lawyer, tries to be sensitive on racial issues. But Saunders came to Charleston in the late sixties to help organize a historically important strike by black hospital workers. I announced to the family that I wouldn't vote, and they never pressured me. Still, during the campaign, I had a sense of lines being drawn. In my confusion I began to hang out with Democrats.

Halloween, three days before the election. The chairman of the Charleston County Democrats is hosting a party. From the outside, his beach house looks as if it had been transported here from Mendocino County. Raw weathered board, stained-glass windows. On the inside the house is grotesque, what my friend Wright called Early Mongoloid.

Wright and I were with two powerful men dressed as pregnant nuns. They carried tapedecks with Gregorian chant music beeping along. Wright wore a debutante's gown. Since I had lived in New York all those years, I wore a cop's shoulder holster, a spiked leather bracelet from a sex shop called the Pleasure Chest, and handcuffs.

At first we had fun. One of the pregnant nuns and I had gone to grammar school together. "But Halloween," Wright remarked, "is when everybody takes off their masks."

I began to realize there were no black people at the party. Then I saw one couple. They weren't in costume. No one was talking comfortably with them. I remembered Maureen's parties in New York, but couldn't think of any way to be friendly without seeming phony.

Then four white people came into the party in blackface. They were disguised as Charleston "flower ladies," black women who line a tourist-trafficked street selling limp flowers to outsiders. "You won bah mah flowah?" the imitators kept saying in what they hoped was Gullah, the black dialect of this region.

I grabbed Wright's arm. "What would you do if you were black at this party?"

Wright grew up in Alabama but she is a peaceful person. "I'd leave."

We went outside. In the chilly air Wright said she thought the Moral Majority was going to make revolution obsolete anyway. On Sunday evenings Wright watches the PTL Club, which broadcasts out of Charlotte. She enjoys seeing Jim Bakker and his wife, Tammy, attack the Humanist Manifesto and the Declaration of Feminism. "The true fuehrer of the right hasn't broken free yet. We're going to have big Mao-like posters of somebody like Jerry Falwell. We're going to have laws making women shave their legs."

Then Wright said, "Okay, you asked me. What would you do if you were a black person here?"

Call it an epiphany. I looked up at the California-style stained glass. "I'd go home and get a gun and blow the windows out of this place."

But we were white, and we went back to the party.

I live in a mansion. I'm the caretaker. Officers' quarters during the Spanish-American War were luxurious, and this house has three floors, seven bedrooms, and wide graceful piazzas all the way around it. Two fountains gurgle in the landscaped yard. There's a library.

When I moved into this house, I loved it. I lay in the master bedroom with the French doors open and the rheostat on the chandelier turned down and listened to the ocean grinding against the beach. I spent lazy hours imagining soldiers pacing up and down the piazzas, formulating strategies.

Then I discovered the servant's room in the basement. Squalid. Cruel. I knew instantly that whoever had lived here was not white. The house began to frighten me.

Willie and I are sitting on the roof, smoking reefer and watching the sunset. I don't ask where Willie lives. The election has been over for several months, and my cousin Glenn beat Saunders so badly he outdrew Reagan.

I want to ask Willie if he knows Topcat Drayton. Topcat Drayton is a black Democratic precinct worker I interviewed on election day. I was fascinated by Topcat, who has a gold front tooth with a star cut into it. Like Willie and me, Topcat's a native.

Bill Saunders had got Topcat into politics. Topcat was proud of her work but even prouder of her two-month-old son, Shaun LaPrince Drayton, sleeping in a crib beside the kitchen table where I had watched her dispensing Saunders flyers to a large group of obedient black children.

Soon after the election, Topcat called to tell me her baby boy was dead. "What you call it, crib death. I hate that name. They have another name I like better, sudden infant, or something. I just wanted you to know."

I want to tell Willie about Topcat's baby, but instead I tell him about my rich aristocratic friend who shot herself. Dixie was drunk and drugged. She'd asked me to go hunting with her that day. Now sometimes I wonder if she would have shot me too. I got to Dixie's house before the ambulance did, and I could have fit my fists into the hole she'd blown through her gut out her back.

Dixie, like her ironic name, didn't die. She said she'd tried to put the shotgun into her mouth but couldn't reach the trigger. I went back to her house the next day and stole the gun. Feelings were running high among her relatives and friends, and I told myself I was helping the gun disappear to protect everyone. But, when I slipped the barrel into my own mouth to see if I could reach the trigger—I could—and hid the gun in the servant's quarters in my basement, I knew my unconscious had sent me a bitter unwanted message. If race war happens in this country I don't know what I'll do, but the luxury of choosing sides may be an illusion. Race, like gender, is irrevocable and visible.

I tell Willie how I knelt, looking into the wide hole where Dixie's load of birdshot had emerged. I don't tell him it reminds me of how I'd once knelt beside a dead man. "Willie, I had to keep telling myself, *This is real.* Because it *didn't* seem real. It seemed like television. War must be like that, like a dream."

"Yeah, war like a dream," Willie said. "War like robbing stores. It sneak right up on you, then you just in it."

The sun is bleeding down the western sky. Willie and I watch while clouds splinter it like horizontal knives. Engorged with red, it drips past the horizon.

"The sun looks awful tonight."

Willie giggles. "You'd hate it more in black and white."

The tension between us is swift, surprising. We crawl to the edge of the roof to gaze down at some carved stone angels guarding the camellias. Willie once gave me a jar of white lightning, and I am telling him the recipe for a redneck drink called Purple Jesus: grain alcohol, vodka, grape Kool-Aid, cherries, and sliced oranges.

"Hey, girl, you want to go out dancing with me some night?"

"Sure." I speak too quickly, wishing I didn't have family all over this city like eyes, wishing I had my anonymity back, wishing I didn't need a past and blood kin.

Willie laughs disarmingly. "Hey, I was just teasing you, white girl."

I don't know what he saw in my face.